W9-BUE-078

THE MIDDLE AGES

Giovanni Caselli

Peter Bedrick Books, New York

First American edition published in 1988 by
Peter Bedrick Books, New York

Published by agreement with Macdonald & Co. (Publishers) Ltd.,
London. A member of Pergamon MCC Publishing Corporation plc.

Library of Congress Cataloging-in-Publication Data

Caselli, Giovanni, 1939–
     The Middle Ages/Giovanni Caselli.
        p.   cm. – (History of everyday things)
     "First American edition" – T.p. verso.
     Summary: Examines daily life in the Middle Ages, covering such
aspects as chivalry, the great cathedrals, medieval technology,
country life, and pilgrimages.
     ISBN 0–87226–176–X
     1. Civilization, Medieval – Juvenile literature
[1. Civilization, Medieval.]   I. Title.   II. Series.
CB351.C29 1988
909.07 – dc19
                                87–27105
                                     CIP
                                     AC

Printed in Great Britain by Purnell Book Production Ltd.
A member of BPCC plc

10 9 8 7 6 5 4 3 2 1

Giovanni Caselli wishes to thank the following people
for their help:

Nicholas Hewetson, artwork preparation
Kareen Taylerson, layout

Editorial and research by
Jacqueline Morley

Introduction

The Middle Ages is a term that suggests an in-between time, between the rational classical world and the intellectual freedom of the Renaissance, when people believed in things and behaved in ways now totally remote from us. They thought, for instance, that people were born with unequal rights, that hours had varying lengths, that in the south the seas boiled. In some cases their facts were plainly wrong, but more often they interpreted them differently because their notions of the nature of the world and the best way to organise society were different from ours. But in their everyday lives they were just like us. This book finds out about the everyday things medieval people did – building houses, going on journeys, playing games, looking after people who were ill – and it brings their activities alive by looking at buildings, tools and clothes they used.

A previous volume in this series, *The Roman Empire and the Dark Ages*, showed how the manorial land-system worked, what life was like inside the monasteries, and how towns came into being. This book takes a longer, closer look at daily life in the Middle Ages. In many ways it was a life that saw startling changes. Ordinary people learnt to read and write; new sources of energy were used, new machines invented; scholars studied Arab scientific writings, traders and missionaries went all the way to China and tropical Africa. Wherever possible this book looks at changes taking place beyond ordinary people's daily horizon – changes which had a lasting effect on what they were able to buy, to do, or think.

Contents

Knights and the crusades	4
The age of great cathedrals	8
The Venice of Marco Polo	12
Medieval technology	16
Country life	20
Trade fairs and markets	24
Entertainmments and tournaments	28
Pilgrims and hospices	32
The court of Burgundy	36
Prosperity in the towns	40
New ideas, new worlds	44
Booklist	48

Knights and the crusades

In the early Middle Ages the source of all wealth was land, worked by peasants. Local lords fought each other to gain land, controlling it with bands of mounted warriors called knights. Fighting on horseback was relatively new; until the eighth century northern Europeans fought on foot. Then they learned from the Arabs to use stirrups which enabled a rider to swing a sword without falling off his horse. For the next seven hundred years horsemen dominated warfare and society.

The feudal system

A lord granted land to enable his knights to pay for horses and weapons. In return they promised to be his vassals and fight for him. Such grants of land were called 'fiefs', and the reciprocal arrangement of knight-service in return for land and protection is known as 'feudalism' (from 'feudum', the Latin for fief). The feudal lord would himself be the vassal of a greater lord, or of the king. At first any man who owned a horse and a sword could be a knight, but in time only the sons of knights were thought suitable. Knighthood became the privilege of a warrior aristocracy, which valued loyalty and courage highly. Its code of conduct was called 'chivalry' (from the French word for a horse). Much medieval warfare involved burning villages and massacring peasants, thus destroying an opponent's means of support.

The knight and his armour

A knight hoped to unhorse his opponent with his lance at the first charge. In close combat he used a sword or battle axe, which cut through chain mail, driving links of metal into the wound. Plate armour was devised to counter this; it developed from small pieces of metal or cuir bouilli (leather boiled in wax and then shaped) placed at vulnerable points, to entire suits of metal. With the rider protected, marksmen aimed at the horse, so this too was given armour.

The decline of the knight

By 1500 armour was perfected, but the knights disliked leaving their estates, and maintaining costly horses and equipment. Instead they paid their overlord to employ mercenaries (hired soldiers), who obeyed no knightly code but fought for anybody. The high cost of mercenaries and modern weapons and artillery meant that by 1500 it was only kings who could afford to make war.

Twelfth-century armour
1 Knight of c.1100. He wears a hauberk of chain mail with an attached head-covering (coif).
2 Saracen warrior. His chain mail hauberk is hidden by a flowing robe.
3 Knight of c.1190. His hands and legs are protected by mail.

Putting on armour: thirteenth century
4 Mail chausses were attached to the girdle which held up the braies (breeches).
5 Putting on the akerton, a padded cloth garment worn under the hauberk. It protected the body from spear thrusts.
6 Under the coif, a quilted arming cap protected the head.
7 Fastening of the chin flap (aventail).
8 Putting on cuisses (padded thigh protectors).
9 A kettle hat. A, went over the coif or a bascinet, B, went under or over it.

Knights of the Military Orders
10 A Hospitaller of c.1250. He wears a cylindrical helmet (great helm) and a sleeveless surcoat. Metal plates (poleyns) protect his knees.

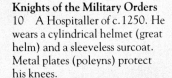

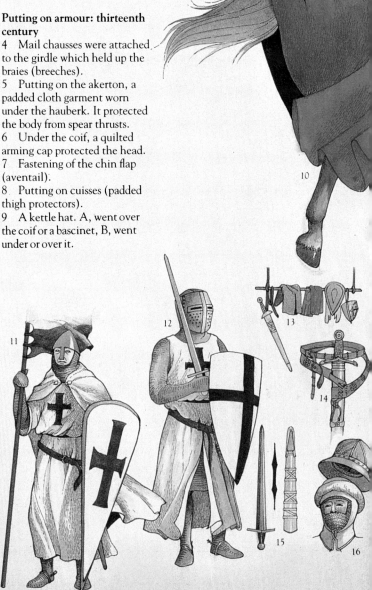

11 Knight Templar, c.1150.
12 Teutonic Knight, c.1250.
13 Equipment hung up at night.
14 Arrangement of sword belt.
15 Sword, cross section of blade, and scabbard.
16 Arming cap with padded roll to support helmet.

Fourteenth-century armour

17 A coat of plates: a cloth or leather garment lined with riveted plates, usually worn between the surcoat and hauberk.
18 English knight, c.1320. His surcoat is cut short in front, showing the coat of plates, short hauberk (habergeon), and aketon below. Plate armour now protects the arms and legs.
19 German bascinet with hinged nose-piece.
20 Bascinet with hinged visor, open and closed.

21 The sword now hangs aslant.
22 English knight, c.1375. The surcoat has become a short tight jupon. The coat of plates and habergeon are just visible beneath.
23 Gauntlet of small plates.
24 French knight, late fourteenth century. The chest plates have united to form a globular, padded breastplate under the jupon.
25 In Germany the jupon was less popular. This effigy reveals the breast plate and skirt of plates.

Fifteenth-century armour

26 Gauntlet with wrist guard.
27 Brigantine of small plates, giving greater flexibility.
28 Complete plate armour, c.1470.
29 Narrow-bladed dagger to penetrate chinks in armour.

FRONT VIEW

REAR VIEW

SWORD POMMEL

HELMET STRAP

DETAILS OF BUCKLES AND HINGES

A holy war

For the medieval knight, loyalty and courage were the highest virtues, and could be put to no better use than in the service of God. In 1095 Pope Urban II called upon Christians to save Jerusalem from the Turks, who had captured Palestine from the Arabs and stopped Christian pilgrimages to the Holy Land. In 1099, after a forty-day siege, crusader forces captured Jerusalem.

Castles in the Holy Land

The crusaders then faced the problem of defending the territory they had taken. In Europe feudal lords had solved this problem by building castles with fortified keeps. The crusaders did likewise, incorporating new defensive techniques learned from the Byzantines and Arabs. They built castles with double rings of protective walls and many round flanking towers. They used machicolation (holes in an overhanging parapet, from which missiles were dropped), portcullises and hairpin entrances. These developments soon influenced the design of castles in Europe.

Warrior monks

The most impressive surviving crusader castle is Krak des Chevaliers, in Syria. Its massive defences were begun in 1110 and extended by the Hospitallers, who owned the castle from 1142. The Knights Hospitallers (later called the Knights of St John) began as volunteers caring for sick pilgrims in Jerusalem. The Pope then recognised them as a religious order of soldier monks. They took monastic vows but were dedicated warriors. Other similar orders were the Knights Templar, established to protect pilgrim roads to Jerusalem, and the Teutonic Knights who fought the heathen Slavs in north-eastern Europe. These orders soon became rich and powerful.

The end of an ideal

Greed for land and spoils, and rivalry among the leaders undermined successive crusades. Venice, which charged for transporting crusaders by sea, demanded a share in their conquests. In the Fourth Crusade, to seek favour from Venice, the crusaders attacked Christians and sacked Constantinople. By 1291 all the land gained was again in Moslem hands.

Despite their failure the crusades had a permanent effect on the way people in northern Europe lived. The crusaders were not interested in the scientific learning of the Arabs, but they were impressed by their civilised life-style. They brought home a taste for eastern fruits and spices – ginger, cinnamon and cloves, figs, dates, sugar, almonds and rice – and for rugs and silk hangings, fine metalwork and glass.

Seige tactics and weapons
1 Undermining defences.
2 An espringale fired darts.
3 Mechanised warfare began with the crossbow. An arrow was released when the trigger was pressed. Crossbows were used in China in the third century B.C. They were used in Europe from the time of the First Crusade.
4 The bowstring was drawn by turning a crank handle.
5 A pavis (shield) protected the marksman while he reloaded.

The first firearms
Gunpowder, also a Chinese invention, was first used by Europeans in the early fourteenth century.
6 A fourteenth-century tormentum, firing darts and stones.
7 A bombard – an early cannon.
8 A fifteenth-century gun.

Storming a fortress
9 Saracen defenders hurl greek fire, an inflammable mixture containing naphtha. The crusaders roll a scaling tower to the walls.

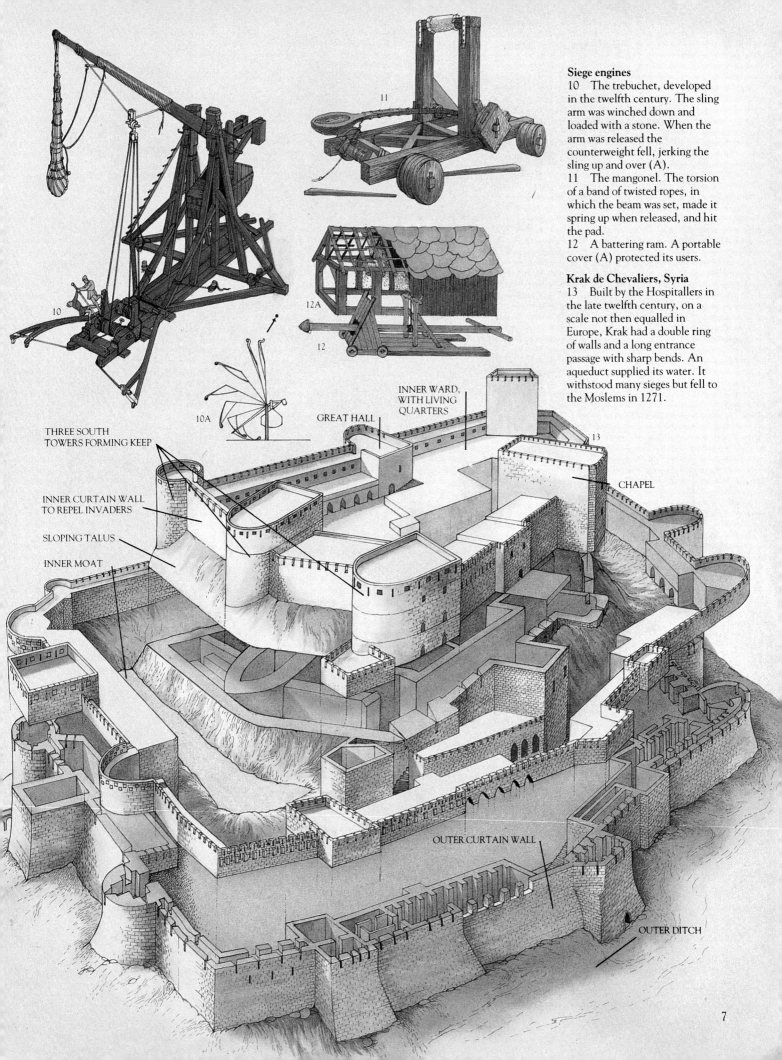

Siege engines

10 The trebuchet, developed in the twelfth century. The sling arm was winched down and loaded with a stone. When the arm was released the counterweight fell, jerking the sling up and over (A).

11 The mangonel. The torsion of a band of twisted ropes, in which the beam was set, made it spring up when released, and hit the pad.

12 A battering ram. A portable cover (A) protected its users.

Krak de Chevaliers, Syria

13 Built by the Hospitallers in the late twelfth century, on a scale not then equalled in Europe, Krak had a double ring of walls and a long entrance passage with sharp bends. An aqueduct supplied its water. It withstood many sieges but fell to the Moslems in 1271.

10

11

12A

12

10A

THREE SOUTH
TOWERS FORMING KEEP

INNER CURTAIN WALL
TO REPEL INVADERS

SLOPING TALUS

INNER MOAT

INNER WARD,
WITH LIVING
QUARTERS

GREAT HALL

13

CHAPEL

OUTER CURTAIN WALL

OUTER DITCH

The age of great cathedrals

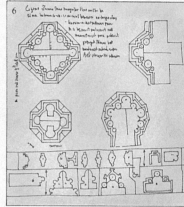

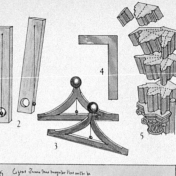

To medieval people a church was not just a place to worship in on Sundays. The church provided them with hope, with guidance and with entertainment. Its stained glass windows and sculptures were their picture book; its festivals and ceremonies delighted them; its buildings were their local meeting places. A cathedral was usually in an important town. The townspeople took pride in their cathedral and raised large sums of money to help build it. The Church taught that such payments helped them to enter heaven.

During the twelfth century a period of magnificent church building began. In about 1140 Abbot Suger of the Benedictine Abbey of St Denis, near Paris, decided to rebuild his church in a bold new style. He wanted it to be light and open, so techniques were used which made it unnecessary to have very thick walls to support the roof. The success of St Denis inspired other buildings in this style, which we now call Gothic. The style spread rapidly to England, and then to the rest of Europe.

The medieval architect

A master craftsman supervised the building of a cathedral. He was what we would now call its architect. He began his training on the site, as an apprentice mason, or carpenter. Plans were drawn at the site, in a special room called the tracing house. Small-scale plans were made on parchment. Details were drawn full-size on the plaster floor, and wooden templates made from them provided the patterns from which the stones were cut. The floor was then rubbed over and re-used.

A thirteenth-century architect's sketchbook

Skilled master masons were in great demand and could find work anywhere in Europe. They kept sketchbooks in which they recorded new architectural ideas that they had seen on their travels. The sketchbook of Villhard de Honnecourt, an architect working in France in the thirteenth century, has survived. He travelled through France, Switzerland and Germany sketching architecture, people, plants and animals. He noted ideas for buildings and statues, and practical tips for other craftsmen: how to make a bridge with timber that is too short; how to measure the width of a stream without crossing it. He drew devices for lifting weights, sawing timber and shoring up leaning buildings. He was particularly impressed by the new cathedral at Laon. He drew one of its towers, from which sculpted oxen gaze out over the town.

A medieval architect
1 An architect confers with his royal patron. From a thirteenth-century manuscript.
2–4 Architects' tools: plumb-lines and set-square.
5 Sections of stone forming a Gothic vault.
6 A page from Villhard de Honnecourt's sketchbook, c.1240, showing sections of piers, and templates for them.
7 The sketch-book is full of lively drawings, like this one of masons playing dice.

Development of the Gothic arch
8 Romanesque tunnel vault.
9 Intersecting tunnels formed groined vaults.

10 Supporting ribs along the groins carried the stonework. Semi-circular diagonals produced a hump-backed vault.
11 To avoid this the smaller arches were made to spring from a higher point.
12 Pointed arches, adopted in the thirteenth century, could be equal in height, whatever their width.
13 Vaulting of Laon nave.

The first Gothic church: St Denis
14 The west front of St Denis (c.1135) near Paris.
15–18 Precious objects acquired by Abbot Suger to adorn the altar at St Denis.

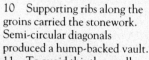

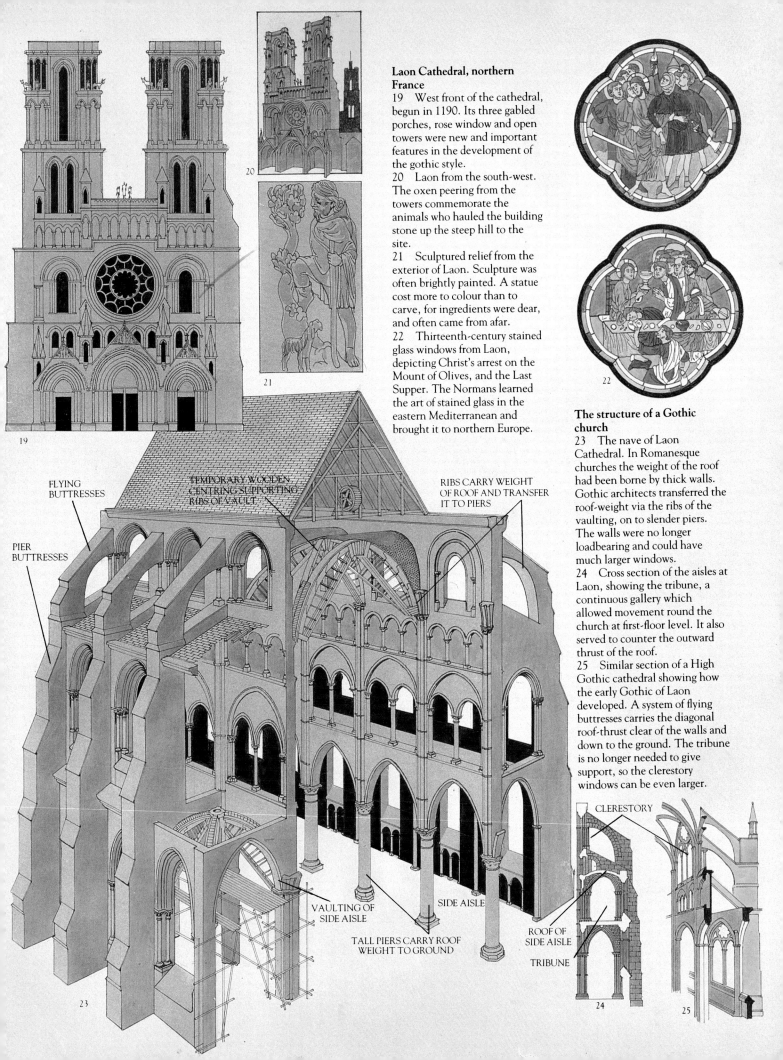

Laon Cathedral, northern France

19 West front of the cathedral, begun in 1190. Its three gabled porches, rose window and open towers were new and important features in the development of the gothic style.

20 Laon from the south-west. The oxen peering from the towers commemorate the animals who hauled the building stone up the steep hill to the site.

21 Sculptured relief from the exterior of Laon. Sculpture was often brightly painted. A statue cost more to colour than to carve, for ingredients were dear, and often came from afar.

22 Thirteenth-century stained glass windows from Laon, depicting Christ's arrest on the Mount of Olives, and the Last Supper. The Normans learned the art of stained glass in the eastern Mediterranean and brought it to northern Europe.

The structure of a Gothic church

23 The nave of Laon Cathedral. In Romanesque churches the weight of the roof had been borne by thick walls. Gothic architects transferred the roof-weight via the ribs of the vaulting, on to slender piers. The walls were no longer loadbearing and could have much larger windows.

24 Cross section of the aisles at Laon, showing the tribune, a continuous gallery which allowed movement round the church at first-floor level. It also served to counter the outward thrust of the roof.

25 Similar section of a High Gothic cathedral showing how the early Gothic of Laon developed. A system of flying buttresses carries the diagonal roof-thrust clear of the walls and down to the ground. The tribune is no longer needed to give support, so the clerestory windows can be even larger.

19

20

21

22

FLYING BUTTRESSES

PIER BUTTRESSES

TEMPORARY WOODEN CENTRING SUPPORTING RIBS OF VAULT

RIBS CARRY WEIGHT OF ROOF AND TRANSFER IT TO PIERS

VAULTING OF SIDE AISLE

SIDE AISLE

TALL PIERS CARRY ROOF WEIGHT TO GROUND

23

CLERESTORY

ROOF OF SIDE AISLE

TRIBUNE

24

25

A cathedral building site

Many of those who gave money never saw their cathedral in its finished glory. During their lifetime work was probably always in progress. The cathedral rose from a muddy building site, amidst saw-pits and hoisting gear. The architect was responsible for organising all supplies, and for co-ordinating craftsmen on the site.

The building rises

First the architect arranged for supplies of stone from the quarry, and for the purchase of timber for the roof. The building lines were then marked on the ground with stakes, rope and measuring rod. Marking out a triangle, with sides 3, 4 and 5 units long, gave a true right angle. Deep stone foundations were laid; sometimes there was almost as much stone below ground as above. Only the outer and inner faces of the church walls were made of stone. The space between was filled with rubble. As the walls rose, scaffolding was erected, and the carpenters made special frames (centring), to support the arch-ribs while the mortar set. During winter, unfinished stonework was covered with thatch to prevent frost damage, and work continued in the covered masons' lodge, on carving details for the window tracery and vaulting.

As the walls neared completion the carpenters prepared the roof rafters and trusses. These were fitted flat on the ground, and then taken apart, each piece being marked for reassembly when it had been hoisted to the roof. Beneath the wooden roof the interior was vaulted with stone. This reduced the risk of fire, and looked more beautiful from within. Gutters and gulleys were finished with lead sheeting, made and fitted by the plumbers. They were shaped like wierd monsters, from whose mouths the rain water shot out, clear of the walls.

All these craftsmen depended on the smith, who made, mended and sharpened their tools. He produced iron claws for grasping weights, nails of all kinds, horseshoes, and tie-rods to stop the walls from spreading. There was a smithy at the building site, and another at the quarry.

The final touches

Decorating the church was very important. Many people could not read and were helped to understand the Church's teachings by pictures and statues of the life of Christ and the saints. In the older Romanesque style of building the walls and vaulting had been covered with paintings. The new large Gothic windows allowed less wall space, so stained glass took over the role of story teller. Statues, both inside and outside the church, were painted and gilded.

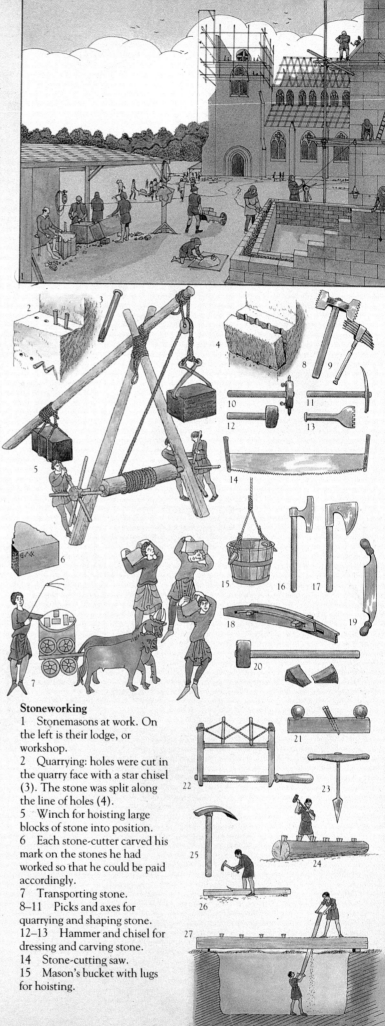

Stoneworking
1 Stonemasons at work. On the left is their lodge, or workshop.
2 Quarrying: holes were cut in the quarry face with a star chisel (3). The stone was split along the line of holes (4).
5 Winch for hoisting large blocks of stone into position.
6 Each stone-cutter carved his mark on the stones he had worked so that he could be paid accordingly.
7 Transporting stone.
8–11 Picks and axes for quarrying and shaping stone.
12–13 Hammer and chisel for dressing and carving stone.
14 Stone-cutting saw.
15 Mason's bucket with lugs for hoisting.

Carpentry

16–17 Carpenters' hammers.

18 Expandable wooden centring.

19 Spoke-shave, drawn towards the user, to smooth a plank.

20 Sledgehammer and wedges for splitting wood along the grain.

21 Plane, known in antiquity but not used in northern Europe till the twelfth century.

22 A bow-saw. The twisted cord increased the blade's tensions.

23 Auger, for boring holes.

24 Splitting a log. Splitting was quicker than sawing, and wood split along the grain was stronger than sawn wood.

25–26 An adze was used to trim the split beam.

27 Sawing a beam into planks.

Glassmaking and metal work

28 Mixing wood-ash and sand for melting in the glass furnace.

29–31 For crown glass, the bubble of molten glass was cut from the blow-pipe, leaving a hole. The hole was widened with a stick till the glass flared into a disc.

32–34 For muff glass the bubble was swung to form a long shape, cut top and bottom, slit length-ways, reheated and flattened.

35 Dividing iron, which cracked the glass with its heated tip.

36 Grozing irons for nibbling the glass to shape.

37–38 Pieces were nipped off till the right shape was made.

39 Lead strips joined the glass.

40 Dividing and grozing iron.

41 Glassworks (fifteenth-century drawing).

42 Soldering bolt for joining lead.

43 Joining sheets of lead.

44 Lead strap to hold sheets.

45 How lead flashing was cut.

46 Flashing sealed junction of roof and tower.

47 Blacksmiths, from a fourteenth-century manuscript.

48 Hinge from Laon cathedral.

49 A master-painter at work. His assistant mixes colours.

50 Constructing vaulting. Stones for the ribs were laid on the centring. The spaces between were spanned by a course of light stones. Materials were lifted by a two-man treadwheel in the roof.

11

The Venice of Marco Polo

During the Dark Ages much of Europe was too unsafe for merchants to travel far with precious goods. The northern Europeans knew little about the skills of other countries. From the tenth century onwards, as communications improved, they began to learn of a far more luxurious world – the eastern Mediterranean, where the Byzantine empire preserved a civilisation inherited from Greece and Rome.

The Venetian traders

Constantinople, the Byzantine capital, was the richest trading city in Christendom, until the thirteenth century, when it was overtaken by the city state of Venice. Venetian ships sailed throughout the eastern Mediterranean and the Black Sea, taking European iron, textiles, and timber on the outward journey and bringing back African gold and ivory, precious stones from Persia and India, and silks, spices and perfumes from the Far East. They brought these goods from Arab trading cities. Some Christians thought it was wrong to trade with pagans, but the Venetians had no scruples about it. The Islamic countries they visited were much more advanced technically than Europe, and Turkish carpets, Persian ceramics and Egyptian and Syrian glass and metalwork fetched high prices in Venice. From there they were traded northwards over the Alps. From the late thirteenth century Venice and her rival Genoa sent fleets of goods twice yearly through the straits of Gibraltar to Flanders and England.

The city of islands

The thirteenth-century Venice that Marco Polo knew, with a population of about 100,000 was one of the largest cities in Europe. Each island was a separate parish with a street plan radiating from its central church and square; even today some bridges cross the canals at an oblique angle because the streets of adjoining islands were not aligned. The main market was at the Rialto, the highest point on the Grand Canal accessible to ocean-going ships. Wooden buildings were replaced, from the thirteenth century, by houses of stuccoed brick, decorated with marble. The wealthiest merchants' houses (called 'palaces') lined the Grand Canal. It was important to have a frontage on the main waterway. Cargoes were unloaded directly into the portico, which led into a large central hall where business was conducted. Away from the main canal stood the houses of lesser merchants and prosperous tradesmen.

1 Venetian doge, c.1300, with staff of office. The office of doge was not hereditary, but was strictly confined to a few merchant families.
2 A young Venetian noblewoman. She holds a fan.
3 A merchant in travelling dress. He is seated in a chair from a thirteenth-century relief on St Mark's cathedral.
4 North Italian thirteenth-century cupboard.

People of Venice from reliefs in St Mark's
5 Boatbuilders. Venice had many shipyards in side canals.
6 Haymaker with scythe.
7 Digger with long-handled spade still used in the Venetian region. Although Venice had to import most of her food there were vineyards and market gardens on the lagoon islands.
8 Grape gatherer with traditional basket.
9 Cooper.
10 Blacksmiths at work.

11 Persian gold and silver inlaid brass casket, early fourteenth century.
12 Egyptian ewer of carved rock crystal of the Fatimid period. Such vessels were highly prized. Many found their way into European cathedral treasuries.
13 Turkish carpet, thirteenth century. Detail of corner with border motifs based on Arabic writing.
14A Syrian glass beaker, gilded and enamelled, c.1260.
B Late thirteenth-century glass with enamelled decoration of saints, probably made in Venice in imitation of Syrian and Byzantine glass. By the thirteenth century pedlars were selling Venetian glass in northern Europe.
15 Egyptian copper basin with inlaid decoration.
16 Persian bowl of Minai ware, interior and side view.
17 Persian lustre dish, late twelfth century.

18   A Venetian trading vessel of the thirteenth century. The triangular (lateen) sails, devised by the Arabs, made boats easy to manoeuvre, which was useful in negotiating coastlines and harbours. Double steering oars were used, although north European ships were adopting the stern-postrudder (the idea may have come from China). The crusaders were taken across the Mediterranean in ships like this.

A thirteenth-century Venetian house

19   House of a merchant or prosperous trader. This drawing is based on a building which survives, with later alterations, in the salizzada (little street) of San Lio. The right-hand tower is conjectural. Main living rooms were on the first floor. The shops were probably let. The large chimney pot stopped flying sparks from starting fires. Most houses had a courtyard with a well, drawing filtered rainwater from an underground cistern. Water from the subsoil was too brackish to drink.

13

Invaders from the steppes

In the thirteenth century Europe was very nearly conquered by people from the steppes of central Asia – the Mongols. These nomadic tribes had been united by a great leader, Genghis Khan. His armies overran much of Asia, India and eastern Europe.

In 1260 Kublai Khan, grandson of Genghis, became leader of the eastern Mongols. He was a man of great vision and very interested in the customs of foreign lands. He brought all China under his rule; his people adopted highly civilised Chinese ways and administered the country well. Their roads were good and travel over the vast empire was safe.

The Silk Road

In Roman times there had been regular trade between Europe and China, mostly in silk. The long trek across central Asia became known as the Silk Road. Merchants did not travel the whole way but exchanged goods at markets along the route. From the sixth century onwards, the Moslems had controlled the western end of the Silk Road. They had kept the precious eastern trade to themselves and stopped Europeans from using the Road. The Mongols had a different attitude. They were not traders by tradition, rather despising such an occupation. When they took over Moslem lands they opened the routes to everyone.

The wonders of China ✡

The Venetians were quick to seize this chance of buying eastern gems, spices and silks. Amongst others, the brothers Nicolo and Maffeo Polo set off to trade with the Mongols of southern Russia. They were invited to China to tell the Khan about the West. Following the old Silk routes they reached the Mongol city of Cambaluc (Peking) in 1266, the first western Europeans known to have travelled so far east. In 1271 they went again, accompanied by Nicolo's young son Marco, whose account of his journey became a medieval bestseller. The Khan sent Marco on missions throughout China. Marco described China's highly developed civilisation, its well-planned cities, excellent roads and canals and extensive shipping, all superior to anything in Europe. Certain outstanding Chinese achievements he did not mention; perhaps he did not grasp their importance. The Chinese had made the first truly mechanical clock in 725 A.D. They invented the magnetic compass and gunpowder. By the eleventh century they were printing from movable type of baked clay.

In 1370 the Chinese drove out the Mongols and ended all contact with the West. Not until the twentieth century was China as open to travellers.

The Mongols, founders of the Yuan dynasty, 1279–1368
1 The Emperor Kublai Khan with a warrior and a woman rider. The Mongols were very skilled horsemen and owed their victories to the terrifying speed with which their mounted archers swept down on the enemy. In their original homeland, on the high plateau of central Asia, they were pastoral nomads who wandered seasonally in search of grazing for their herds of sheep, cattle and horses. Some of their descendants still live in this way today.

The Mongols' movable house
2 The Yurt. The collapsible framework, A, made of rods and lattice of willow, was covered with felt lashed with horsehair rope. B A rug covered the doorway. C The roof dismantled. D The whole yurt went on the back of a camel.
3 Two pairs of Mongol gold earrings.
4 Gold tablet of the kind which the Polos were given by the Khan as a safe-conduct pass through Mongol lands.
5 Two bronze Nestorian crosses. Some Mongols were Nestorian Christians.

The skills of thirteenth-century China

6 Porcelain vase, Yuan dynasty. The secret of making porcelain was never revealed to Europeans.
7 Teapot in shape of wrapped bundle, Chi-chou ware.
8 Cup and saucer in the form of a paeony, celadon ware.
9 Stoneware jar, Tz'u-chou ware.

10 Sung celadon bowl.
11 Spouted dish, interior and side view, early Yuan porcelain.
12 Silk weaving. The silk worm had been domesticated since at least the fourteenth century B.C. but the Chinese guarded the secret closely. Silkworm eggs were smuggled from China in the sixth century A.D. Inset: thirteenth-century Chinese twill silk damask.

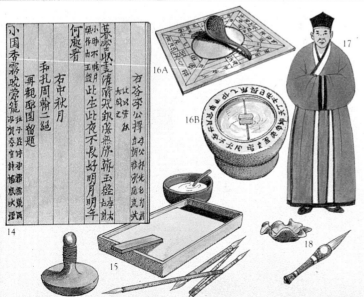

13 The China Marco Polo saw based on a scroll painting.
14 Poem printed in 1213 from moveable blocks.
15 Block printer's tools.
16 Magnetic compass.
A Compass used from the fourth century B.C., for magic purposes: a bronze plate with a spoon of magnetic lodestone.
B Ninth-century mariners' compass, used from 9th century: a floating magnetised needle.
17 Scholar of Yuan period.
18 Scholar's paint brush, and brush basin in shape of a lotus.
19 Chinese women, late thirteenth century.

15

Medieval technology

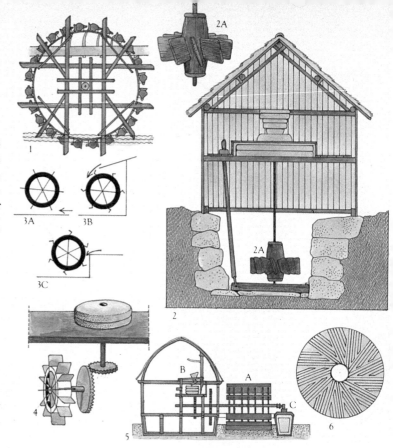

Medieval people were just as inventive, and just as unwilling to do hard work if they could use machines instead, as we are today. Machines using cogs, gears and pulleys were known in the ancient world but they were mostly used for making toys. There was plenty of slave labour to do the heavy work. Medieval scientists and engineers made machines do the work of men. Machines need a source of power and the first to be widely used was water.

Water and wind power

The Romans had used waterwheels but they were not very effective in countries where rivers dried up in summer. Water power came into its own further north, as work and trade expanded, from the tenth century onwards. The mill usually stood on a river bank but it could also float in midstream or be moored under a bridge to take advantage of currents between the piers. Projections, called cams, were added to the shaft of the waterwheel. As the shaft turned, the cams raised levers which operated hammers, enabling all manner of pounding jobs to be done. Mills could grind flour, crush olives, full cloth, tan leather and pound pulp for paper.

The importance of iron

Most medieval machine parts were made of wood because iron was so expensive. Water power improved metal-working techniques and made iron cheaper. Stamping mills crushed the iron ore and trip hammers did the smith's hardest work. Water-powered bellows produced draughts strong enough to liquify ore. The first European blast furnace recorded was working in 1380.

The European windmill was invented in the twelfth century, although another type already existed in the Near East. Windmills were built wherever there was no fast flowing water. Not freezing in winter, they were especially useful on the northern plains of Europe.

Wind or water could turn wheels round, and the cam shaft could lift hammers which dropped again by their own weight, but it was difficult to turn rotary (round and round) motion into reciprocating (backwards and forwards) motion. In the fifteenth century the crank and connecting rod were invented, which turned rotary movement into reciprocating movement or vice-versa. The greater availability of iron made this possible, for wooden parts would have been worn away by friction.

Watermills
1 A noria, the oldest type of waterwheel.
2 A horizontal water-mill. The water-wheel A moves the millstone directly.
3 How the water turns the wheel: A undershot wheel; B overshot wheel; C breastwheel.
4 The Romans used gears to make the millstone turn faster than the wheel.
5 Section through a floating mill: A waterwheel; B millstones; C feed hopper.
6 Millstone. As the upper stone turns on the lower, the grain is sliced by the crossing grooves.

Windmills
7 Persian windmill. Section showing vertical shaft and horizontally rotating vanes.
8 Cross section showing how walls admit prevailing winds.
9 Fifteenth-century drawing of post-mill with hoist for raising grain.
10 A tower-mill. Only the cap, bearing the sails, rotated.
11 Interior of a post-mill.

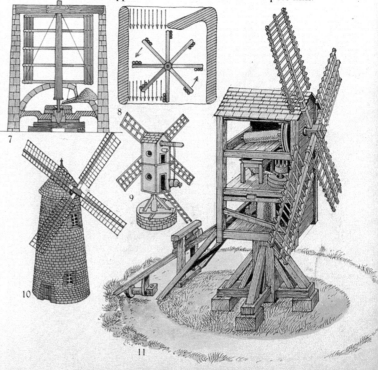

Lifting gear

12   Treadmill crane at Bruges.
13   Slewing crane, from a manuscript, c.1430.
14   Villhard de Honnecourt's drawing of a screw-jack for raising heavy loads.
15   Cutting a screw. Villhard's sketch shows a gauge notched at intervals which are thirds of a rod's diameter. A The rod is marked from the gauge. B A cord wound through these points shows where the screw must be cut.
16   Villhard de Honnecourt's machine for cutting piles under water. A saw in a frame is positioned over the pile and its height adjusted at the top of the frame. Two men guide the blade. Pressure comes from a stone mounted on a wheel.
17   Machine for boring tree-trunks to make water pipes, from a drawing of c.1430.
18   Reconstruction of machine.

Reciprocal motion

19   Simple crank-handle, from a ninth-century drawing.
20   Hand-mill with crank and connecting rod, from a manuscript of c.1430.
21   Mill with a double crank and connecting rod, treadle-driven, from the same manuscript.
22   Villhard de Honnecourt's drawing of a power saw. A cam-shaft depresses the blade and a spring-pole raises it.

23   An Italian architect, Giovanni da Fontana, proposed this self-driving carriage, c.1410.
24   Medieval industrial building c.1250. Originally a smithy and metal workshop, it forms part of the Cistercian abbey of Fontenay, Soane-et-Loire, France, and still stands today. The Cistercians, wanting to be self-supporting, always chose sites with a good water supply which they diverted to drive machinery for many uses. All over Europe Cistercian monasteries had industrial buildings like the one shown here.
25   Plan of a typical Cistercian monastery based on that at Clairvaux, showing how water from the river was used for sanitation and to power mills for many purposes.

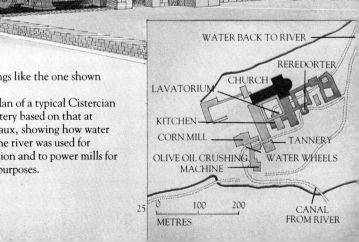

WATER BACK TO RIVER
REREDORTER
CHURCH
LAVATORIUM
KITCHEN
CORN MILL
TANNERY
OLIVE OIL CRUSHING
MACHINE
WATER WHEELS
CANAL FROM RIVER

25

0   100   200
METRES

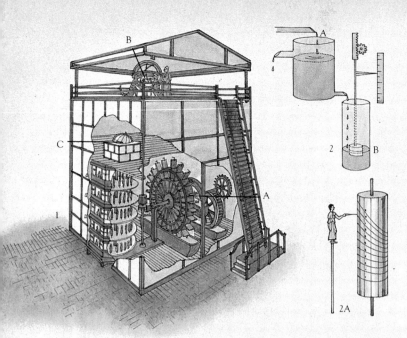

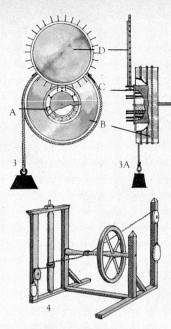

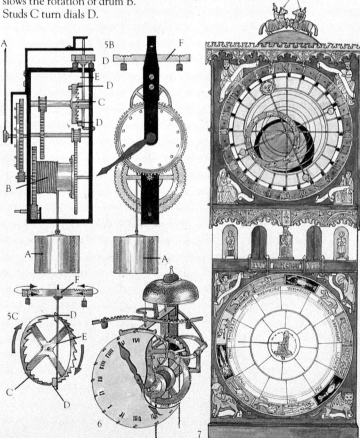

The sun as a clock

For thousands of years people regulated their lives by the sun. In early medieval times the monastery bell was the only measure of time ordinary people heeded. The monks' hours were elastic, for they divided the day into twelve hours of daylight and twelve of dark, so summer daytime hours were longer than winter ones.

Sun and water clocks

Sundials are the oldest clocks, but when the sun was not shining the monks used a water clock. Its time keeping was governed by the rate that water leaked from a jar.

The demand for accurate timepieces came from astronomers who wanted to reproduce the motion of the sun and the planets, which is the basis of accurate timekeeping. They required a wheel which could turn slowly, yet constantly, once every twenty-four hours. Water clocks could not be accurately controlled, and in winter they froze.

The invention of mechanical clocks

The first mechanical clock was made in China in the 8th century A.D. An even more famous astronomical clock was made by Su Sung in 1092. Although driven by water power these were not water clocks, for they possessed an escapement – a device which holds back the clock's driving force, allowing it to 'escape' slowly and regularly. Clockwork was not developed for everyday use in China because the making of astronomical instruments was a closely guarded 'official secret'.

Clocks change society

In the earliest European mechanical clocks power was supplied by a falling weight and the escapement which

1 A reconstruction of Su Sung's astronomical clock. A waterwheel A provides power to rotate a planetarium B and a celestial globe C, and to move the figures which appear in openings to mark the passage of time.
2 Water clock. Overflow pipe A ensures equal water pressure so that float B rises evenly.
2A Indicator for hours of variable length.
3 Mercury escapement, an Arab device, from a book of c.1276. Mercury trickling through pierced partitions A slows the rotation of drum B. Studs C turn dials D.

3A Side view.
4 A primitive escapement from a drawing by Villhard de Honnecourt.
5 Clock with verge escapement. A side view; B front view; C detail of escapement. A falling weight A turns drum B. The motion is transferred by gears to the escape wheel C. The rotation of this wheel is constantly halted as its teeth engage with first one, and then the other, of two projections (pallets) D on a rod (the verge) E. As each pallet is pushed aside the verge pivots, and its crossbar (foliot) F, with hanging weights, is swung back and forth. The resistance of these weights interrupts the turning of wheel C and slows the fall of weight A.
6 Monastic alarum clock, c.1380. Knobs set in the rotating dial lifted a lever which operated the alarum. This warned that it was time to toll the bell to wake the rest of the monastery.

Public clocks
7 Some clocks had elaborate dials with clockwork figures that moved on each hour, like this, c.1380, on Lund Cathedral, Sweden. It tells the date and days of the week.

8 Town clock on the belfry of the market hall at Bruges, as it looked in the fifteenth century.
9 Watchman's horn.
10 Striking mechanisms were often made in the form of the bell-ringing watchmen they replaced.

11 Wrought iron mechanical cock from Strasbourg cathedral clock, 1354. At noon it crowed, spread its feathers and flapped its wings. A, B and C details of mechanism.

12 Giovanni de' Dondi showing his clock to nobles of Padua, c.1365. It took him sixteen years to make and attracted astronomers from all over Europe.

Spring-driven clocks
13 Leonardo da Vinci's sketch of a fusee, c.1490.
14 Reconstruction of a clock with spring and fusee, from a manuscript of 1477. The tapering shape of the fusee A compensated for the diminishing power of the unwinding spring B.

15 Portable spring-driven clock, from a mid-fifteenth century painting.
16 The oldest surviving spring-driven clock, c.1430.

slowed its fall was in the form of a 'verge and foliot'. This device appeared in the late thirteenth century. By the mid-fourteenth century many monasteries, cathedrals and town belfries had a mechanical clock which struck the hours.

The invention of the spring-driven clock, during the fifteenth century, enabled rich people to have small portable clocks. The watchman who blew a horn from the town gatehouse or rang a bell from the belltower to mark the old-fashioned variable hours became an outdated figure. The regular striking of the public clock synchronised people's actions. Measuring time gave rise to the notion of saving it, of making things faster so that they could be sold with more profit, and of doing things to a deadline. Thus the competitive modern world was born, where success is measured in terms of this world and not of the next.

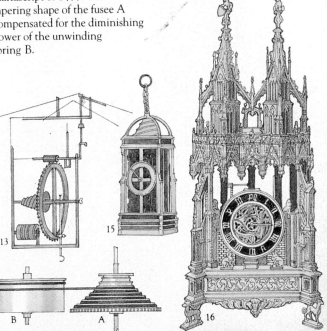

Country life

Medieval countryfolks had to rely on their local soil, good or bad, to provide them with food, clothing, warmth and shelter. The same land could not feed both people and animals at the same time. The problem lay in finding the best balance between them, for without animals the fields could not be ploughed or manured. Over the centuries various solutions were handed down as farming custom from one generation to the next. A broad distinction can be made between the farming that resulted in northern and in southern Europe.

Farming in northern Europe

Heavy northern soils needed to be ploughed with a heavy plough in order to dig deeply and provide drainage. The land was ploughed in long strips because turning the oxen was cumbersome and slow. In order to share good and bad land equally each peasant's holding was made up of long and narrow scattered plots in open fields. The villagers had to agree to grow the same crop on all the strips of a field.

The land was kept fertile by resting it for a year and by putting animal dung on it. The simplest scheme was to divide in two the land used for crops and let alternate halves lie fallow. Population growth in the twelfth and thirteenth centuries meant more grazing land was cleared for crops. There still had to be enough grazing left for the animals, who provided plough teams, clothing and manure. Another solution took advantage of the moist spring weather. The same amount of land was made more productive by dividing it in three. A third was sown in the autumn with winter wheat, a third in the spring, with barley or oats, and a third lay fallow. Animals grazed on the fallow and on the stubble after the harvest was cut.

A different system for southern Europe

In southern France, Spain and Italy, lighter soils and summer droughts produced different crops and field patterns. A light plough and spade was all that was needed to work the soil. The plough was simply made and could be pulled by one ox, so a moderately wealthy peasant could own his own plough and be independent of his neighbours. He could enclose his land and grow whatever suited him. There was not enough spring rain for a second grain crop, so Mediterranean farmers relied on olives, vines and fruit trees. Pasture was poorer than in the north so there were fewer animals. In places flocks were driven long distances to find summer grazing.

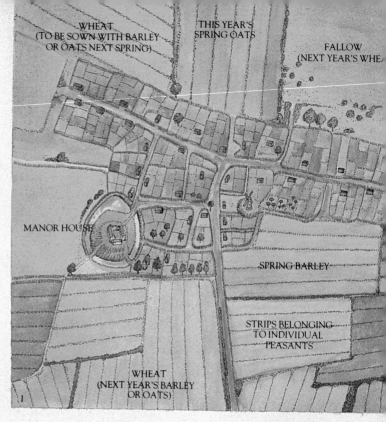

1 A northern European settlement, based on excavations at Goltho in Lincolnshire. The enclosures, or crofts, around the houses contained open cattleyards. Tofts for growing vegetables extended beyond them to the open fields. The plan of Goltho is fairly typical, though many factors, such as the lie of the land or the need not to build on good farmland affected the way a village grew. Some faced inwards round a green; some straggled along a road.

2 A southern European settlement, the hill top village of Montefioralle, Tuscany. The pattern of closely grouped houses, forming a protective wall, in the midst of tilled fields, was usual until the introduction of the 'mezzadria' (crop sharing) system by which some peasants became part-owners and overseers and lived in farmhouses on the land. A local market was held at the point where the road from the village crossed the river.

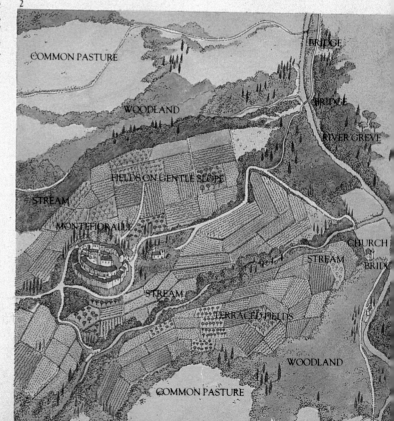

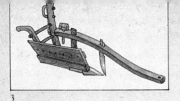

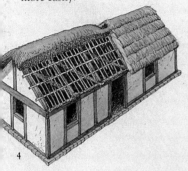

3 The heavy northern wheeled plough with coulter and mouldboard. The coulter cut vertically through the soil and the ploughshare cut horizontally. The mouldboard turned the slab of soil to one side, forming a ridge and furrow which helped surface moisture to drain away more easily.

4 Reconstruction of a house at Goltho. The timber framework is wattle-and-daub, and stands upon stone footings. It would probably have lasted about fifty years before needing to be rebuilt. This type of building, divided by a cross passage into dwelling quarters and a byre or storeroom, is known as a longhouse. It was the home of a fairly prosperous peasant. The poorest villagers lived in cots which were smaller, with little room for storage, and none for animals.

5 The light southern plough only scratched the surface of the soil, but that was all that was needed to work the light earth into a fine powder.

6 A Tuscan farmstead, adapted to hilly ground. Animals were stabled on the ground floor.

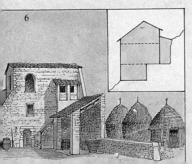

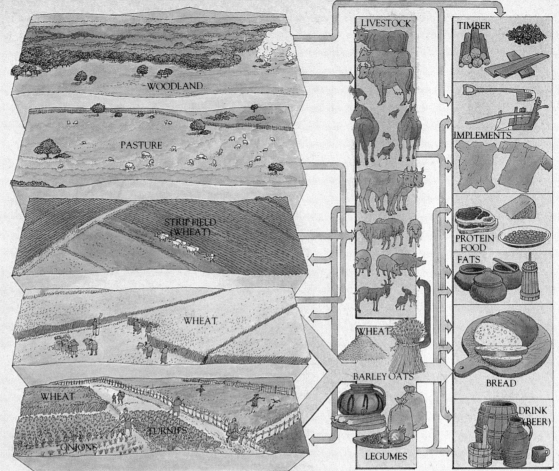

7 Northern cultivation. Cereals are important for food and for brewing ale. Animals supply most fats and proteins.

8 Mediterranean cultivation. Fewer animals are kept. Olives and nuts provide fats and proteins. Woodland is important in both economies, providing wood for tools and housebuilding, fruit and nuts for food, and acorns for pigs.

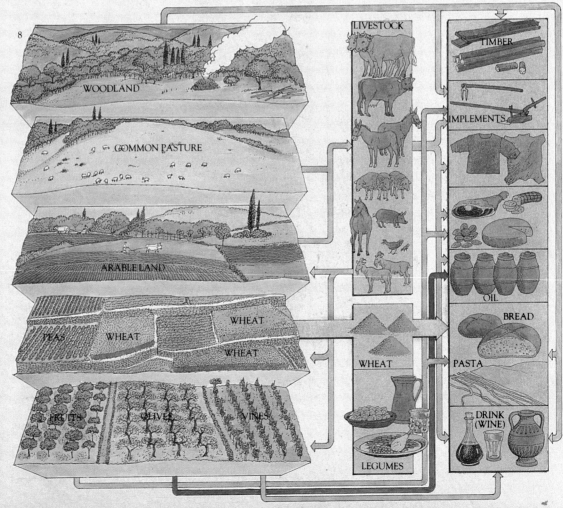

The visit of the lord of the manor

In northern Europe the typical country community was the manor. The manor house was the centre of a self-supporting estate. The lord of the manor might hold land in various parts of the country which he visited in turn. Whenever he arrived, with his family and large train of servants, he found all the food that such a large household needed, ready and waiting for him, due to the hard work of his peasants throughout the year.

Penhallam Manor

At Penhallam, Cornwall, archaeologists have uncovered the remains of a manor house, abandoned in the mid-fourteenth century. These show the arrangements awaiting the visit of lord of the manor. They were more comfortable than those of Norman times. Instead of being in scattered timber buildings linked by covered passageways, the stone-built hall, chamber, kitchen and service rooms were interconnecting and placed around a courtyard. The wardrobe, a most important part of a medieval house, was on two floors. The upper was used for sewing and for storing clothes; the lower was for storing valuable household things: cloth, silk and rare imported foods (almonds, sugar, ginger). Another important room was the brewery. People avoided drinking plain water for they knew that it could make them ill. Brewing, which involved boiling, was safe, and ale was everyone's daily drink.

The farming year

While the lord came and went the peasants were tied to the routine of the seasons. In the new year animals which had been grazing on last year's stubble were driven off and ploughing began. Seed was scattered by hand with broad sweeps of the arm, and the harrow was dragged across the land to cover it. The corn was hand-weeded as it grew. June was haymaking time. The lush rivermeadows reserved for hay were protected by a special officer, the hayward. He looked after the movable hurdles which kept the animals out of the meadows and cornfields, for there were no hedges. Hay was cut close to the ground with scythes, and gathered up and stacked with long wooden rakes and pitchforks. From August onwards the corn was harvested. Unless straw was needed for thatching the ears were cut off high up, leaving plenty for grazing. The corn was tied into sheaves and carted home for threshing during the winter months. Then the fallow field, which had been ploughed during the summer, was sown with winter corn. The hayward let the animals on to next year's spring cornfields and fallow, and the year began again.

Fourteenth-century costume
1 The lord of the manor and his wife, c. 1360.
2 A girl and a youth, c. 1340.

Work on the manor: scenes from the Luttrell Psalter, an English manuscript of c. 1340.
3 Using the heavy plough.
4 Breaking clods of soil.
5 Casting from a seed lip.
6 Harrowing to cover the seeds.
7 Reaping and binding corn.
8 Carting home the sheaves.
9 Threshing corn with flails to separate grain from husks.
10 Milking sheep in a fold made of movable hurdles. Women carry away crocks of milk.
11 A beehive. Honey was the main sweetener. Sugar was a luxury imported from the Arab world.
12 Herding geese.
13 Women used every spare moment for spinning. This one has not put down her distaff while she feeds the hens.
14 A travelling carriage. The household was often on the move, as its lord visited his various manors. His womenfolk might use such a carriage. Men rode, and the furnishings and equipment went on carts and pack animals.

15 Penhallam Manor, Cornwall
The house was built in three stages, from c. 1180–1236. The oldest room is the chamber, over an undercroft. It belonged to an earlier hall and was for the lord's private use. The wardrobe, with garderobe (lavatory) attached was added to it. Then a new hall (the main living and dining room) was built, and joined by a covered passage to the chamber. A service wing, comprising buttery and servery, combined bakehouse and brewhouse, pantry and kitchen, adjoin the hall. Rooms above the buttery may have been for the oldest son, the steward, or the chaplain who officiated in the private chapel. South of the kitchen are lodgings for retainers or guests. These are provided with garderobes, which drain into the moat. No trace of window glass has been found, although it was just beginning to be used in English houses when Penhallam was built. The hall windows had wooden shutters which bolted. The stable and perhaps a dovecote would have stood outside the moat. Inset: the drawbridge mechanism. A counterbalance prevented the bridge from crashing down as it was lowered.

14

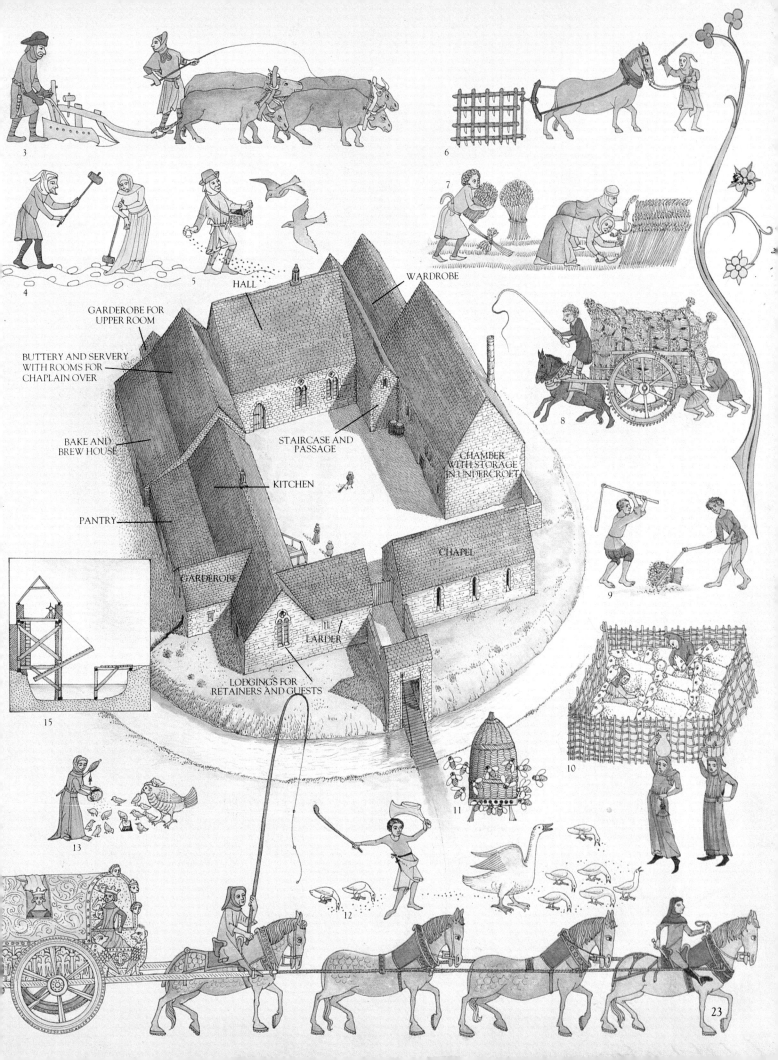

3

6

4

5

7

HALL

WARDROBE

GARDEROBE FOR
UPPER ROOM

BUTTERY AND SERVERY
WITH ROOMS FOR
CHAPLAIN OVER

8

BAKE AND
BREW HOUSE

STAIRCASE AND
PASSAGE

CHAMBER
WITH STORAGE
IN UNDERCROFT

KITCHEN

PANTRY

9

GARDEROBE

CHAPEL

LARDER

15

LODGINGS FOR
RETAINERS AND GUESTS

10

11

13

12

23

Men and women at the Champagne fairs, c.1275
1   Merchant wearing a garde-corps with hanging sleeves.
2   A Florentine merchant.
3   Parisian cloth merchant.
4   The cloth merchant's wife.
5   Women buying eggs.
6   Shops of (left to right) the twelfth, thirteenth and fourteenth centuries, from remains at Cluny, France.
7   Italian money changers. They set up a trestle table with a cloth upon it. This was the 'banco' from which the word 'bank' is derived.
8   Furriers. Furs from northern Europe were an important item of trade.
9   A hosier's stall. Fashions changed slowly in medieval times, but the fairs catered for those who could afford to be fashionable.

Trade fairs and markets

The last chapter of *The Roman Empire and the Dark Ages* described how markets began, at places where country people came to exchange produce, and how towns grew up around markets. When travelling merchants from different countries gathered at convenient markets to exchange goods those markets grew into international trade fairs. The fairs were encouraged by local rulers because they made money from the renting of stalls, the taxing of sales, and the letting of land.

A European centre

The most famous trade fairs were those of the Champagne region of north-eastern France, where trade routes from all the lands of Europe crossed. In the late twelfth and thirteenth centuries they were the main European centre for the exchange of goods. French and Flemish merchants came to sell their cloth, mostly woven from fine English wool. The Italians came north to buy it, for it was one of the few European products coveted by the middle-eastern merchants who supplied them with the pepper and spices they brought to the fairs. They also brought oriental and Italian silks, alum and rare dye-stuffs needed by the northern cloth makers, and cotton fibre, used not for weaving but for padding armour and quilts. Leather goods came from Spain and furs from north-eastern Europe. Local lords sent their stewards to buy a year's supply of weapons, cloth, spices and sugar. Taverns, street entertainers and local traders flourished. Merchants from the leading trade cities had permanent halls in which they displayed the goods they brought to sell.

The organisation of fairs

Trade fairs were strictly organised. Superintendants, with a staff of clerks, inspected goods and sales. Disputes were settled in the fairs' commercial courts. In England these were called 'piepowder' courts, because the travelling merchants were called 'pieds poudreux' – dusty feet. The Champagne fairs had a timetable. Each of the six fairs lasted for almost two months, forming a continuous year-long market. For the first week the merchants set up their stalls in allotted places. Then there was a twelve-day cloth fair, followed by an eight-day leather-and-fur fair, and lastly a fair for everything that was sold by weight. Reckonings were made in local money; after the cloth fair the money changers were allowed to trade for a month, so that merchants could change their profits into the coin of their own country.

10 A butcher's shop. The fairs served as local food markets.

11 A grain chandler. Wheat was an important commodity.

12 The town weighmaster checked that goods sold were of true weight.

13 Thirteenth-century steelyard weights.

14 The object to be weighed was hung from the shorter arm, and the weight was slid along the other till they balanced.

15 Fourteenth-century 4-ounce weight.

16 Stacking weights of the late middle ages.

17 Weighing with a bismar. The cord was slipped along the beam until it hung horizontally. The position of the cord indicated the weight of the object.

18 A grain measure, pivoting to measure various amounts.

19 Tally sticks. The larger piece was a receipt and the smaller a copy.

20 Medieval Bar-sur-Aube, site of one of the Champagne fairs.

21 The fair at Bar-sur-Aube in the fifteenth century. The shelter for merchants remains today.

CHURCH OF ST PIERRE WITH MERCHANTS' ARCADE

CHATEAU (MERCHANTS OF YPRES AND CAMBRAI LODGED IN THIS AREA)

Safe travel

The counts of Champagne wanted to encourage the fairs; they took special care to protect merchants travelling to them by maintaining the roads in good repair and getting neighbouring lords to guarantee the safe conduct of merchants passing through their lands. This was vital, because travel was hazardous for men and for goods. Highway robbery was common, attacks by wild animals were a possibility, and there was always the danger that a ruler with a grievance against a foreign state would seize its merchants' goods as a reprisal.

Following the old routes

Most merchandise travelled north–south through France and along the coast of Italy, or on narrow mule-tracks over the Alpine passes. The roads often followed the old Roman routes but in many places these had deteriorated to dirt tracks. Local rulers were responsible for roads through their territory, but upkeep was very patchy. Toll bridges were sometimes built by royal command, or by monasteries wanting to help pilgrims on their way, but there were many streams with only dangerous fords to cross by. Travellers to out-of-the-way places needed a guide for there were no signposts; country people did not need them and probably could not have read them anyway.

Well-to-do people travelled on horseback. On long journeys they could hire fresh mounts at relay stations. Everyone else went on foot. Merchants rode in groups for safety, leading long trains of packmules. As roads improved horsedrawn carts began to replace animals. A merchant convoy covered about thirty kilometres a day.

The importance of waterways

Goods were sent by water wherever possible, despite the danger from storms and pirates, for it was cheaper than by land. When the Genoese and Venetians began to send regular merchant fleets to northern Europe instead of using the French roads, the Champagne fairs lost their international trade. Inland waterways were widely used and large trading cities grew up beside important rivers. London and Paris are examples. A good bridge and a quay were essential for the prosperity of such towns. Early bridges were usually built of wood, but wherever possible they were replaced by stone. These were fireproof and less liable to be swept away by floods. They often had a chapel on them, with its own priest who might collect donations from passers-by for the upkeep of the bridge. Bridges were expensive to build and costs were recovered by letting the space upon them for building shops, or beneath them for watermills.

Life on the bridges of Paris
Scenes redrawn from the borders of illuminations in a French manuscript of 1317, which tells the life of St Denis, the patron saint of Paris, in over sixty scenes. Each scene is bordered by a deep frieze showing various kinds of traffic on and under the bridges of Paris.

A frieze of selected scenes
A shepherd with his flock is followed by a cart laden with sheaves of corn.

On the water men are preparing to unload two boats of firewood while another has moored his boat and is having a siesta.

A performing monkey; a man and woman driving laden mules; children playing see-saw on a wheelbarrow.

On the river: boats with awnings, of the kind used for transporting corn; a boatload of melons.

Each frieze is different. The gates, watchtowers and shops on the bridges are schematically drawn, though it is clear that the roadway is paved. In contrast the activities on and under the bridges are realistic and vivid. Above: A pilgrim; a swineherd; a porter; a woman riding side-saddle; a birdseller with a goldfinch in a cage; a leper; a blind man with his dog; a man goading a donkey; a cripple; a street brawl; a shoemaker's shop; a porter; and a beggar. On the river a man fishes and a fresh-fish seller is trading from his boat. Floating mills are moored under the arches.

Two porters trudge along with heavy bundles while two noblemen on horseback enjoy a discussion. Below them, a swimming party; some people are getting undressed. Two boats of coal are delivered. Four men find it hard work to pull a wine cask; two others are transporting a heavy load on wheelbarrow. A baker's boy is delivering bread; a milkman shoulders two pails; below them fishermen haul up their nets.

A man driving cattle is followed by a covered carriage with passengers and a youth with a pair of greyhounds. Below them, a man with two boats of wine in casks is paying tax to an official of the port of Paris. Another tests the wine. A cartload of paving stones and a troupe of entertainers: a performing bear does tricks while a woman dances. On the river: a passenger offers his fare to a ferryman; corn is brought to be ground at one of the many mills under the bridge.

27

1

Entertainments and tournaments

Medieval people had many holidays to look forward to. All these, except May Day and the New Year, celebrated religious festivals. The number of festivals grew until there were up to fifty a year, plus Sundays. These were holidays without pay, so for really poor people they may have been a mixed blessing. All work stopped, and after everyone had worshipped in church and watched the big church procession, they had the rest of the day to enjoy themselves. They sang, danced and drank ale, and watched the travelling performers who came to town – jugglers, acrobats and tightrope walkers, and men leading performing bears or monkeys. Sometimes plays were performed in the streets, usually with a religious theme. They had begun in the early middle ages as church performances which dramatised the meaning of the service. By the thirteenth century they were being held out of doors as well, on wagons or trestle stages.

The annual fair

Every town and village had its own special holiday on a feast of a patron saint, or for an annual fair, usually held on a saint's day. Some towns had a horse race through the streets, or a kind of football game in the town square. Archery, wrestling and fighting with long staves were also popular. Gambling games were forbidden by the church, but most people took little notice. Dice games were the commonest form of gambling. Cards appeared in the fourteenth century, but card games did not become really popular until printing produced packs with identical backs.

The art of falconry

Most country sports were forbidden to working people; wild animals belonged to the lord who held the land and poaching was severely punished. Many hunting manuals were written in the fourteenth century, explaining the correct methods for hunting various animals: deer, boar, bears, fox and hare. Falconry was the noblest form of hunting. An animal on the ground could be chased and cornered, but birds which could fly beyond arrow range were difficult to catch. Falcons were trained to swoop on them and strike them down. They were then retrieved by dogs. A trained falcon was more precious than a hunting dog. Knights and ladies carried their favourite about with them and placed them behind their chairs at meals.

Falconry
1 Falconers, from an Italian manuscript, c.1260.
2 Training a falcon to return to a lure of crane's feathers.
3 Falcon's bell. Attached to the bird's legs these told where it was when high out of sight.
4 In the early stages of training, and when being moved, the birds were calmed by having their eyes covered by a hood. The falconer kept hold of the tail of the hood to prevent the falcon removing it.
5 Linen bag for handling falcon, from manuscript, c.1260.
6 Falconer's purse for the bird's reward of chicken.
7 Settling falcon on a perch.

Boar hunting
8 Ivory hunting horn.
9 Boarhound's collar to protect its throat from the boar's tusks.
10 Huntsman's knife.
11 Boar spear.
12 Boarhunt, from the Book of the Chase, by Gaston Phebus, 1387.

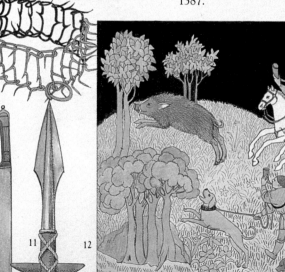

Children's games
13   Pottery doll and rider.
14 and 15   Toys from a fourteenth-century manuscript: windmill and battledore-and-shuttlecock.
16   Bowling a hoop, fifteenth century.

Players and entertainers
17   Glazed pottery whistle.
18   A psaltery, played by plucking with the fingers.
19   Bagpipes.
20   The vielle, with one or more strings, was played with a bow.
21A & B   Street performers.
22   Stiltwalker.

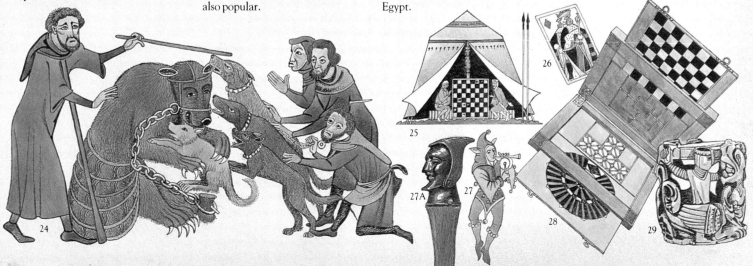

Mummers
23   Masked mummers, from a fourteenth-century French manuscript. They are taking part in a 'charivari'. The tradition of mumming, in which masked countryfolk performed plays and dances, was very old. Many of the performances were based on pre-Christian rituals.

Animal baiting
Many medieval sports would be thought cruel today. Country people had to work so hard that they had little thought to spare for the feelings of animals.
24   Bear-baiting, from the fourteenth-century Luttrell psalter. Cock-fighting and, in some regions, bull-baiting were also popular.

Indoor entertainments
25   A Christian and a Muslim playing chess. Chess probably originated in a sixth-century Indian game and was brought to Spain by the Moors.
26   A fifteenth-century knave of diamonds. Playing cards seem to have originated in the east and to have reached Italy from Egypt.

27   A jester, kept as part of a lord's household staff, to amuse him whenever he wished.
27A   Head of a jester's bauble.
28   A fifteenth-century folding set of boardgames.
29   A thirteenth-century chessman. Chess pieces gained their present form in the fifteenth century.

The ritual of the tournaments

The ceremonies he describes are very elaborate. They began many days before the tournament itself, with the sending of a challenge from one great noble to another. The king-at-arms then proclaimed the tournament far and wide, inviting nobles to attend. On the opening day judges and contestants rode into town in formal procession; the banners of the chief knights were hung from the windows where they lodged. On the second day the helms of the contestants were displayed, so that the ladies might inspect them, and denounce any knight guilty of an unchivalrous act. On the third day a 'chevalier d'honneur' was chosen. During the contest he carried a handkerchief upon a lance and any knight he touched with it was spared further attack. On the fourth day the tournament was held, followed by the awarding of prizes. Each day ended with feasting, music and dancing.

The medieval tournament

The tournament was a sport for nobles only, though everyone watched who could get a viewing point. This ancient war game grew in popularity in the twelfth century. Early tournaments were real fights, with very few rules. The loser surrendered horse and harness and had to pay a ransom. Some knights became professional players. The English baron William Marshal won twelve horses at one tournament, and he and a companion took 203 knights in a season; he hired two clerks to keep check of his earnings. After one victory he was discovered with his head on a blacksmith's anvil, having his battered helmet hammered straight, to get it off.

The church opposed tournaments because they were dangerous. Rules were introduced to make the game safer. Three types of tournament were recognised; one in which weapons of war were used; one in which the contestants wore 'arms of courtesy' designed not to wound, and a compromise type in which real weapons were used but the fight could be stopped at any moment. Personal quarrels were often settled like this. Later tournaments featured the joust, a clash between two knights who tried to unhorse each other with their lances. In the fifteenth century a long barrier or 'tilt' was introduced. The combatants rode on either side of it.

As knights became less important on the battlefield the tournament ceased to be a training ground for war and became pure pageantry. In about 1460 King René of Anjou wrote a book describing the proper way to hold a tournament. These illustrations are based on those in his book.

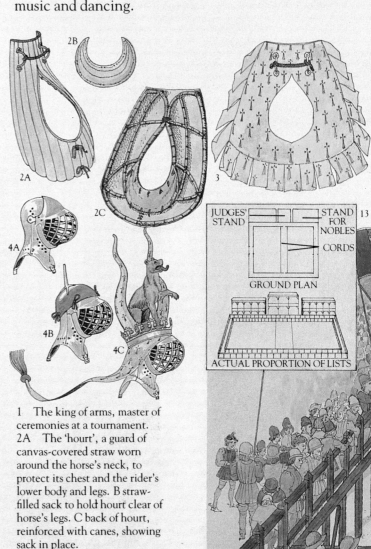

1 The king of arms, master of ceremonies at a tournament.
2A The 'hourt', a guard of canvas-covered straw worn around the horse's neck, to protect its chest and the rider's lower body and legs. B straw-filled sack to hold hourt clear of horse's legs. C back of hourt, reinforced with canes, showing sack in place.
3 Armorial cloth which covered hourt.
4 Fixing the crest. A bascinet. B Cuir bouilli cap. C crest attached.

King René described each item of equipment. Weapons were designed not to inflict serious hurt. They had to be inspected by the umpires.

5   The cuirass, pierced with holes to lessen its weight, was large enough for a padded pourpoint to be worn beneath.

6   The shield, held by cords, was notched to accommodate the lance.

7   Cuir bouili armguards. Tournament armour was of cuir bouilli or metal.

8   The wooden mace, with leather covered handgrip, was worn suspended from a hook on the right breast of the cuirass.

9   The sword had no point or cutting edge. It was attached to the wrist by a strap.

10   Light wooden lance with metal tip.

11   Lance tips were splayed so that they did not pierce armour.

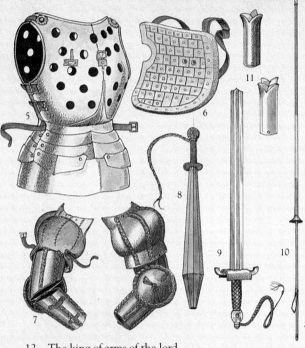

12   The king of arms of the lord challenging, displays the coats of arms of eight nobles, from which the lord defending is asked to choose four umpires. This lord wears a Portuguese fringed hat.

13   The knights have entered the tournament ground, or lists, and the contest is about to start. Pages with raised axes await the signal to chop the cords. Then the knights will rush forward.

The umpires occupy the centre stand, with the ladies of the court on either side. This is based on King René's manuscript. Inset: plan of the lists.

Pilgrims and hospices

Travelling to see holy places is a very old custom. By the third century pilgrims were going to Rome, and to Jerusalem by the fourth. Every object associated with Christ or his Saints was holy, so the possession of a relic made a church into a pilgrim shrine. The most revered places were Rome, Jerusalem and Santiago de Compostela in Spain, where the bones of St James had been discovered in the ninth century.

A pilgrim's dress

A pilgrim was blessed by his priest before starting his journey. In the early days he wore a coarse woollen gown and a hood or round felt hat. He carried an iron tipped staff with a knob or handle. He leant on this as he walked and used it to ward off dogs and wolves. From his staff hung a leather-covered water bottle. His scrip (a purse for receiving alms) was attached to his belt or hung from his shoulder. If he was going to the Holy Land he wore a cross upon his robe. On the journey home he sewed an emblem on his hat or purse to show where he had been. Pilgrims returning from Santiago wore cockleshells; from Rome a pair of crossed keys or a vernicle (an image of St Veronica's handkerchief impressed with Christ's features); from Jerusalem a palm leaf.

The dangers and the pleasures

The journey had its dangers and discomforts. Half a metre of sleeping space per person was marked out on the underdecks of pilgrim ships sailing to the Holy Land. A fifteenth-century guide told travellers to buy bedding for the boat before leaving Venice; it could be sold back on return for half the price. They were also advised to take a chest with a lock, a frying pan, wooden platters and a bread rasp (for grating hard bread).

A pilgrimage could be an enjoyable holiday, especially when people journeyed in a large party. There were plenty of inns on pilgrim routes. Some people travelled very comfortably, on horseback with a retinue of servants. Many made a round trip to several pilgrim cities, sight-seeing and collecting souvenirs. They had to be told how to behave in the Holy Land – not to write on walls or break off pieces of stone. A man complained to the Archbishop of Canterbury about rowdy pilgrims 'with bagpipes, and sound of singing and jangling of their Canterbury bells, they make more noise than if the king came with all his clarion and many other minstrels'. The archbishop sided with the pilgrims.

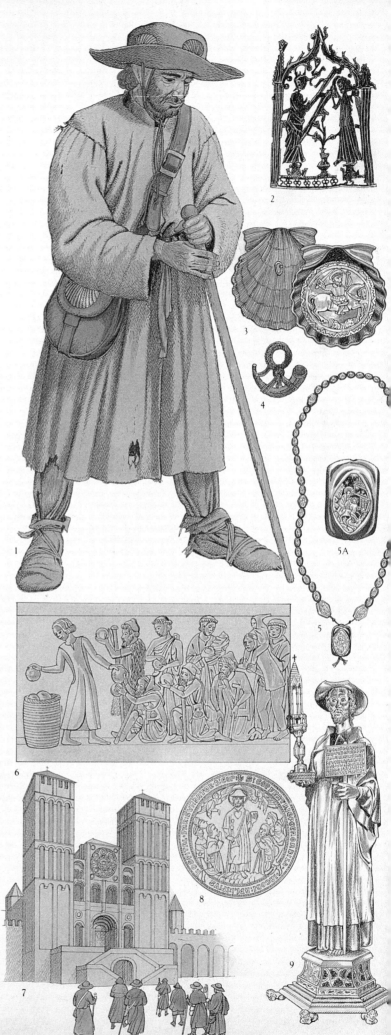

The pilgrim

1　A pilgrim who has been to the shrine at Santiago de Compostela. He has the badge of St James in his hat. Some pilgrims made their journey out of love of God, some went to give thanks for a prayer answered, and some were sent by the church, to show their repentance for a sin.

2–4　Pilgrims' souvenir emblems.

5　A fifteenth-century English rosary of enamelled gold. Rosaries were among the souvenirs sold to pilgrims. They were usually worn around the wrist or at the girdle. Beads of different shapes or colours represented the various prayers to be said. A centre bead with Virgin and Child.

The pilgrimage to Compostela

6　Stone relief of poor pilgrims being given bread, from a tomb at Leon cathedral, Spain.

7　The west front of the cathedral at Compostela, as it was in the late twelfth century. It was rebuilt after being burnt by the Moors in 997.

8　Seal of the Brotherhood of St James, a group of charitable societies which raised money to build churches and bridges, and to found hospices, along the pilgrim routes to Compostela.

9　Fourteenth-century statue of St James from the cathedral of Compostela. A reliquary was the container in which a relic was displayed. Churches competed for relics because they brought special blessings and were an enormous tourist attraction.

10

The journey

10　Pilgrims paying tolls, from a fifteenth-century manuscript. Pedlars of souvenirs were not the only people to make money out of pilgrims. Lords of the lands they crossed sent agents to collect fees.

11　The main pilgrim routes.

12　Pilgrims praying at a shrine, from a thirteenth-century manuscript. A guide points out the sights and a custodian guards the shrine. Sick pilgrims, hoping to be cured by touching the saint's coffin, are crawling through special openings in its outer case. If an object was found, or saved, through prayers to a saint, it was customary to measure it and to burn a thanksgiving candle with a wick of that length before his shrine. If the object was big the wick was wound into a coil.

13　Shrine of St Osmund, Salisbury, with similar openings.

Canterbury pilgrims

14　Fourteenth-century devotional card sold to pilgrims.

15　Pilgrim's badge of St Thomas of Canterbury.

16　Canterbury pilgrims from a fifteenth-century manuscript. Left: the hospice of St Thomas, Canterbury.

PILGRIMAGE ROUTES TO SANTIAGO DE COMPOSTELA AND ROME AND THE HOLY LAND

LONDON
CANTERBURY
FALMOUTH
SOUTHAMPTON
REIMS
PARIS
ORLEANS
TOURS
VEZELAY
BOURGES
SANTIAGO DE COMPOSTELA
PERIGEUX　LE PUY
PADUA　VENICE
PUENTE LA REINA
BURGOS
TOULOUSE　ARLES
MEDITERRANEAN SEA
ROME

11

12

14

15

13

16

1

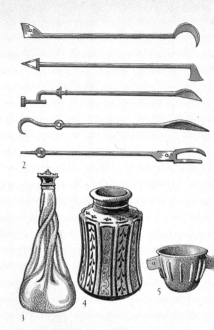

The surgery and its equipment
1   A doctors' surgery, from a fifteenth-century manuscript. One doctor lets blood from a patient's arm. Another inspects a flask of urine brought to him in a covered basket. Inspecting urine and blood-letting were doctors' commonest techniques.
2   Dental tools. Doctors provided fillings and artificial bone teeth for the rich. Poor people went to a tooth-drawer at the fair.
3   Glass apothecary's bottle, fifteenth century.
4   Thirteenth-century drug jar.
5   Bronze mortar for grinding medicine herbs and drugs.
6   Listening to a patient's chest, fourteenth century.

Hospices for pilgrims

The church provided lodgings for pilgrims in hospices along the pilgrimage routes, where they found free shelter, food and bed. The word 'hospice' (hospital) originally meant a place where guests were received. The church's hospitality also extended to the old, the needy and the sick in mind and body. Hospices were established by bishops or religious orders, and administered by monks and nuns, with lay people to do the manual work.

The earliest hospitals

Hospices were not hospitals in the modern sense. Prosperous people who fell ill were nursed by their families and perhaps visited by a doctor. The church's hospitals looked after those who were too old or too ill to earn their living by begging.

The earliest hospitals contained a single large ward, used for living, eating, sleeping and worship. Sick people were washed on admittance and their clothes disinfected. They were bathed regularly, their hair washed and their sheets changed.

The inmates of hospices for old people remained there for the rest of their lives. Men and women lived in separate institutions with little privacy. By the fifteenth century they were housed in almshouses, often founded by guilds or by rich citizens.

Doctors and surgeons

The church looked after the sick, but it was not interested in medical science. Skilful doctors and surgeons were scarce and expensive. Most of their knowledge came from Greek and Arabic writings. They could set fractures and perform successful operations on the body and skull. They attempted to anaesthetise patients by putting sponges soaked in opiates to their noses.

In the face of infectious illnesses doctors were more helpless. In the early Middle Ages the most feared was leprosy. Leper houses were built beyond city walls, usually close to the road so that passing travellers could give alms. A leper had to wear distinctive clothes; he was forbidden to walk unshod, to wash in a spring or stream, or to enter a church, mill, bakehouse or tavern.

Leprosy had become rarer by the fourteenth century, but the plague arrived to take its place and was much more horrific. After the Black Death lingering outbreaks were controlled by isolating sufferers in special hospitals, called pest houses.

7A

7

7   Cupping, from a fifteenth-century woodcut. The skin was scratched and a glass cup, whose air had been heated by a flame, was placed on it. As the air cooled blood was drawn into the glass. A cupping glass.
8   Probing a plague sore.

6

8

Medicine and hygiene

9 An English thirteenth-century diagram of the bloodstream, derived from Arab sources. European medicine was indebted to the Arabs who had inherited classical and ancient Egyptian medical traditions.

10 Washing hands before a meal. Although people did not understand the nature of germs they were careful to eat with clean hands.

11 Clearing out a cesspit, from a fifteenth-century drawing. It was believed that 'bad air' caused disease and attempts were made to keep it sweet. Where lavatories could not be built over running water, a cesspit was often dug, usually under the cellar floor with a pipe to a lavatory above. Men were hired to empty it when full.

12 A wooden lavatory, opening out of an upstairs room, with a walled cesspit below, from a fifteenth-century manuscript.

Leprosy

13 A leper, from a thirteenth-century manuscript.

14 A leper's clapper.

15 A leper's begging bowl. The amber in the bottom was thought to have healing properties.

16 Leper's crutches to help in crawling on the ground.

The hospice at Beaune, France

17 Stretcher patients are being carried across the courtyard from the main ward to the sick rooms. The hospice was founded in 1443 and stands today.

18 Aerial view.

19 Ground plan: A great ward; B sickrooms; C kitchen; D pharmacy; E nuns' refectory; F passage to garden.

20 Hospital ward, from a fifteenth-century manuscript. It was not uncommon to have more than one in a bed.

ceremonies which foreign ambassadors had to attend. The duke's state bed had blankets of ermine lined with lilac silk, and sheets of embroidered Brabant linen.

Patronage of the arts

In addition to encouraging craftsmen, the dukes of Burgundy were great patrons of the arts. The best musicians, poets and painters north of the Alps were attracted to the Burgundian Court. Jan Van Eyck was court painter to Philip the Good. It was thought proper for nobles to have literary interests and to write love poems. Philip the Bold formed a literary society called the Court of Love at which noblemen and women gathered to debate and to exchange poems. Prizes were given for the best ballads.

The court of Burgundy

In 1363 the King of France granted the wealthy duchy of Burgundy to his second son, Philip the Bold. By marrying Margaret of Flanders, Philip also became master of most of present-day Belgium and the Netherlands. For the next hundred years Philip and his successors, John the Fearless, Philip the Good and Charles the Bold, ruled over the richest and most dazzling court of Europe.

Displays of wealth

The Burgundian court was extremely formal and ceremonious, and lavish in its display of wealth. Tapestries, gold and silver vessels and jewellery in huge quantities were commissioned from the finest French and Burgundian craftsmen. On every possible occasion Philip the Good paraded his entire court in costume of the utmost luxury. This display was not the result of childish vanity, but a deliberate show of strength. The more clothes a lord could supply for his retainers and the more gold dishes he displayed on his buffet (side table), the more powerful he was thought to be. When Charles the Bold entertained the Emperor Sigismond the buffet held 136 silver and gilt ewers and flasks, six gilt nefs and many smaller bowls and cups. Beside it stood six unicorn horns (in reality narwhal tusks, thought to be a protection against poisoning) said to be 'beyond price'.

Under Charles the Bold rigid ceremonial increased. He spent enormous sums on the upkeep of his household, which had a hierarchy of officials, each of whom was governed by the strictest rules of etiquette. The duke's dressing and undressing became formal

1   The chateau of Saumur, France, built c.1400 by the Duke of Anjou. The castles of the dukes of Burgundy have not survived but they must have looked very like this. In the foreground is a tilt yard.
2   Philip the Good, Duke of Burgundy from 1419 to 1467. He stands under a canopy of state.
3   Arms of Philip the Good.
4   Insignia of the Order of the Golden Fleece. To revive chivalrous ideals, Philip the Good created a new knightly society, the Order of the Golden Fleece, in 1429. The privilege of belonging to the order was coveted by the nobles of Europe.
5   Silver-gilt cross, on which the Knights of the Golden Fleece swore their oath of loyalty.
6   Enamelled beaker. The patronage of the Burgundian dukes encouraged the most exquisite jewellery and goldsmithing.
7 & 8   Brooch and hat pendant belonging to Philip the Good.
9   Links from a Burgundian chain of office, gold.

A picnic party at the Burgundian court

From a painting of c.1415. The duke and his courtiers are enjoying refreshments during a hunting expedition. The duke has decided that everyone should wear white on this occasion, though fur, velvet and gold embroidery make the effect as sumptuous as possible. The women wear full-skirted overgarments (houppelandes), which reveal their underdresses at the neck. Most of the men wear houppelandes to the knee, with wide elaborately dagged sleeves and capes. The man in the right foreground is showing the pourpoint, with bombard sleeves, which was worn beneath. The men's hair is shaved away below the tips of the ears; the women's is bound up in nets in the form of two horns. Both men and women wear elaborate hats. Some of the women wear bourrelets (a kind of padded turban) decorated with falling fringes of pinked cloth, in imitation of the male fashion of tying and draping the hood around the head instead of wearing it in the normal way. (The duke, leaning against the table, has done this.) Some of the men have hats of beaver felt – a special weather-proof kind came from Germany – and others wear straw hats, which began to be imported from Italy at this time. The popular shape is wide-brimmed, with a pork-pie crown, but the man next to the duke has a tall-crowned hat of a shape that was becoming fashionable. The men wear hose with fitted soles and some have long pointed clogs. Both men and women wear long decorative chains which must have been difficult to keep in place.

The ceremonial dinner

The ceremonial surrounding the serving of a great lord's dinner was always elaborate, and at the Court of Burgundy especially so. The procession of dishes was led in by the Grand Master of the Palace, bearing his staff of office. Every dish was tasted before being presented to the duke. The chief carver touched the carving knife with his lips and kissed the duke's napkin before he used it. The large ceremonial salt cellar was set in the middle of the table and covered with a napkin. Beside it were placed the duke's bread, rolled in two napkins, and his goblet, also covered. The cupbearer and breadmaster carried napkins over their shoulders while they served the duke, but had to lower them to their arms when they moved to persons of lesser rank. The salt cellar was sometimes hung with 'serpents' tongues' (in reality fossilised shark's teeth), with which the duke's food was tested for poison. If anything poisonous was placed near it the tooth was said to sweat.

The table was laid with two cloths, an under one, richly embroidered and reaching to the ground at both ends, and an upper one along the top of the table only. While hands were being washed the cloth was protected by a 'sanap' – a long wad of several thicknesses of linen which was stretched along the table's edge and afterwards removed.

Since knives and spoons were the only eating implements the role of the carver was most important. Fish and meat had to be small enough to be eaten with the fingers of one hand. Ordinary people ate their meat on trenchers, made from slices of a special hard bread. Great lords had trenchers of gold or silver, round or oblong. While the meal was in progress officials of the dining room stood by the side dresser, to give out and take back spoons, cups and plates and to pour out wine according to orders brought by those waiting at table.

The kitchen

Meanwhile in the kitchen the master-cook sat on a high stool between the serving table and the fireplace in order to supervise all stages in the preparation and presentation of the meal. In one hand he held a large spoon, partly for sampling dishes and partly for controlling his large staff. In the vast kitchen, with three huge double fireplaces, which Philip the Good installed at his town house in Dijon, twenty-five people were employed as cooks, storekeepers, stokers and fuel attendants, polishers and apprentices. Adjoining the kitchen was a 'paneterie' (pantry) where bread was stored and a 'fruiterie' where not only fruit was kept, but also wax for candles and torches, and candlesticks and other lighting apparatus.

The kitchen of the dukes

1 The great kitchen at the palace of the dukes of Burgundy, Dijon. It was built for Philip the Good and still stands.
2 Cross-section of the kitchen showing central flue which drew away heat and cooking fumes. A detail of stone ribbing at the base of the ventilating flue. B ground plan of kitchen: a oven; b fireplaces; c cooking range; d well with water supply to kitchen.
3 One of pair of andirons supporting logs for fire, and spit for roasting. Container A for hot embers, was set in cradle of andiron and cooking pots were kept hot on it. B hook for cooking implements.
4 Pewter drinking goblet.
5 Copper basin, tin-lined.
6 Hanap, or shallow drinking cup, of pewter. A cross-section.
7 Pewter serving dish. One dish was set between two people who both ate from it. A cross-section. Pewter cups and dishes were stored in leather bags.
8 Nutcrackers.
9 Turning the meat on the spit.

A lord's tableware

12 Set of four table-knives, with enamelled and gilded handles, made for the father of Philip the Good. Such sets were looked after by the carver, who wore them in the hanging case and brought them to the table when the lord was seated. The larger knives were used by the carver and the smaller by the lord. The posts of carver and cupbearer (who supervised the serving of drink from the sideboard) were important, and held by nobles. They can be seen in attendance on the Duke of Berry below.

13 Covered ewer of agate, mounted in silver-gilt. Precious pieces like this had specially made leather cases for storage.

14 A nef – an ornamental dish in the form of a ship – was a symbol of high status used only by very great lords. It was placed to the left of the host and contained his dining utensils and napkins. This one is formed from a nautilus shell, elaborately mounted.

15 Mazer, a wooden drinking vessel, of silver-mounted boxwood.

16 Ceremonial salt cellar, agate and crystal, gold mounted. It could also be used for spices.

17 A pair of gilt flasks for wine and water.

18 Enamelled silver spoon, front and back view.

19 Silver beaker.

20 Oyster knife with folding blade.

Serving the feast

10 Musicians in the gallery.

11 The Duke of Berry, Philip's great-uncle, entertains (from his Book of Hours, c.1416). The chamberlain, with staff and chain, greets new arrivals who warm their hands at the fire. A firescreen shields the Duke. The tapestry and canopy of state have been folded up over the chimneypiece.

one for carts. On two sides of the inner courtyard is an open portico where carriers delivered goods and visiting merchants showed their wares. The living quarters are on the far side of the court. Jacques Coeur planned them carefully for they are conveniently arranged. Kitchens, reception rooms and private rooms are inter-communicating yet self-contained, with their own entrances and staircases.

The merchant class liked to display its wealth in fine houses, luxurious furnishing and in rich clothes. The elaborate ornamentation of Jacques Coeur's house proclaims its owner's success. On the facade, a pun upon his surname (which means 'heart') is contained in the motto which boldly declares 'to a valiant heart nothing is impossible'.

Prosperity in the towns

Medieval people thought that each person's place in the world had been decided by God. Society, they believed, was made up of three groups: nobles, clergy and peasants. Each group had duties towards the others: the nobles to defend them, the clergy to look after their souls, and the peasants to grow their food. In early medieval times most people fitted roughly into these categories. The growth of trade created a new class, the burghers, or town dwellers. The townspeople made bargains with their feudal overlords which bought them rights to self-government.

The selfmade man

Through trade townspeople could acquire money and power, no matter how humble their origins. Rich merchants often lived more luxuriously than nobles. One of the most outstanding self-made men of the late middle ages was the Frenchman Jacques Coeur who made a fortune trading with the East and became finance minister to Charles VII. He was a merchant on the grandest scale, lending 200,000 gold crowns to the king in 1449 for his wars against the English. Jacques Coeur's enemies, fearing his power, accused him of embezzling the king's revenues; the king seized his goods, and banished him from France.

A merchant's house

At the height of his fortune Jacques Coeur built a magnificent house in his native town of Bourges. Though few people lived so splendidly the house had much in common with those of other merchants. It was both home and office. The imposing street frontage has two entrances, one for pedestrians and

THESE THREE TOWERS WERE ORIGINALLY PARTS OF RAMPARTS OF TOWN

APARTMENTS

BANQUETING HALL WITH GREAT CHAMBER ABOVE

40

A merchant and his wife

Costume of wealthy townspeople of northern Europe in the mid-fifteenth century.

1 The woman's overdress is open to her high belted waist and the underdress is low at the throat. Her sleeves are set in, not cut in one with the garment as before. Her starched veil is supported by wire and held in place by many pins. In 1391 the Queen of France bought 8,900 English pins for her head. Since then veils had been getting higher and airier.

2 The man is dressed in the style Jacques Coeur would have adopted. He wears a chain of office and a large jewel in his hat. The drapery of his hat is derived from the fourteenth-century hood with a long tail, or liripipe. The length of his fur-lined pelisse denotes status and dignity.

Jacques Coeur's house

3 Stone relief of a ship above a doorway. Jacques Coeur owned many ships which sailed from Aigues-Mortes in southern France to trade in the eastern Mediterranean.

4 Jacques Coeur's motto.

5 Three trees over an entrance symbolise his trade with the spicelands.

6 View of the house.

7 Plan of the ground floor: A kitchens; B banqueting room; C covered galleries; D apartments. Heat from the kitchens provided steam baths on the floor above. A trap door in the banqueting-room floor allowed wine to be brought chilled from the cellars. Over the banqueting room was a great reception room, and in the tower at its corner were Jacques Coeur's private office and treasure chamber.

8 A stone servant looking out of a false window of stone.

Wealthy furnishings

9 The fireplace in winter. A larger settle is placed in front of the hearth. Its back rest pivots so one can face either way. A table was put before it at mealtimes so that the master and mistress could dine cosily.

10 The fireplace in summer. A curved fitted chimney-board keeps out draughts.

11 Brass chandelier. Its height is adjustable.

12 Armchair with storage space under its hinged seat.

13 Mirror. The frame is enamelled with scenes from the life of Christ.

14 Chest for storing linen and clothes. It could be covered with cloth and cushions and used as a seat.

15 Folding table, from a Flemish painting. An Italian jug of tin-glazed earthenware and a book in its cloth cover rest upon it.

16 A merchant counts his money, from a fifteenth-century drawing.

17 Small wooden coffer for money or valuables.

18 A folding stool. Seats on this principle had been made for centuries.

SERVICE WING WITH APARTMENTS ABOVE

GALLERY

CHAPEL

MAIN ENTRANCE

DISHES PASSED THROUGH HERE

SERVING ROOM

MINSTRELS' GALLERY

WELL

SERVICE COURT

GREAT COURT

A

A

B

C

C

MAIN STAIR

FIREPLACE

WARDROBE

D

D

MAIN ENTRANCE FOR HORSES AND WAGONS

CONCIERGE

KITCHEN ENTRANCE

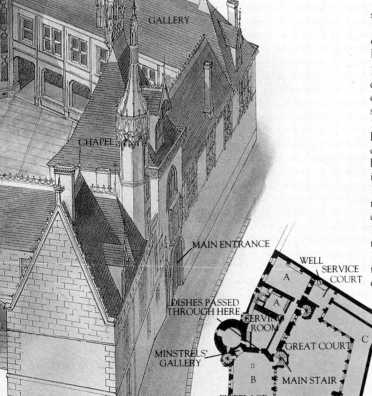

A wife's duties

A late-fourteenth-century French book of household management describes how the home of a wealthy burgher was run. Its author, known as the menagier (householder) of Paris, was a rich elderly man with a very young wife. Girls had to marry the man their parents chose, so this difference in age was not as uncommon as it would be today. The menagier's book of instructions was written to make sure that his wife would do him credit when she was widowed and remarried.

The menagier begins with his wife's moral duties. She must get up early and say her prayers. She must dress suitably, without 'too much or too little show', taking care that her shift and underdress do not ride up at her neck and that her hair does not escape from her wimple. When she goes out she must be accompanied by her housekeeper–companion. She must walk with lowered eyes and speak to no one in the street. To her husband she must be loving, humble and obedient.

Then the menagier turns to practical tasks. His wife must know how to garden and how to manage servants. She must consult her steward about the hiring of day labourers and tradesmen, and her housekeeper about choosing domestic servants. Housework must begin early; all the rooms must be swept, the stools and benches dusted and the cushions shaken into place. Her maids must regularly clean, air and mend the sheets, dresses and furs. The menagier gives advice on removing grease spots, catching fleas and keeping mosquitoes out of the bedroom. Most important, she must see that the kitchen is kept clean and that proper dinners are ordered.

The rights of women

The menagier evidently had a large household, and a house in the country as well, for he gives advice about overseeing the farm hands 'when you are in the village'. His wife would not have had to do the housework herself; she was an administrator in charge of a large staff and her husband expected her to be efficient. Women were believed to be inferior to men and could show their abilities in a restricted way only. Their legal status varied; in some regions they could not inherit land, make a will or be a witness in court. The right to inherit land, which began to be recognised in the thirteenth century, enabled women to be sovereigns in every European country except France, though they could not hold any other public office. In the towns women had more freedom. They could trade in their own right and form guilds. In thirteenth-century Paris these included embroiderers, seamstresses, spinners, woolcombers, hatters, provisioners and doctors.

1 Mistress of the house instructs her steward.
2 & 3 Plants trained in the shape of a nef and a crown.
4 Fifteenth-century garden, from a Flemish painting. Inset: watering can, detail of base and section. It was plunged into water and the hole covered by the thumb. Water flowed from the base when the thumb was lifted.

5 Room in the house of a prosperous burgher in northern Europe in the fifteenth century, from Flemish paintings. A midwife is showing a new-born baby to its mother. Her friends and servants are preparing to bath the baby in a big metal basin of a kind that was in common use for stand-up washes, etc. One woman hands a towel from the chest where linen is kept; another tests the heat of the water with her hand; she has put on a waterproof cuff to protect her sleeve. The end curtains of the bed, which can be drawn to keep out draughts, have been pulled up into a neat hanging bundle for daytime. The ewer and basin in the alcove and hanging towel beside it are for washing hands and face. The window has glass in the fixed upper pane only. The gap below is filled by two sets of shutters which can let in varying amounts of light and air. The openwork panel at the bottom does the work of a modern net curtain and safety rail.

Articles used by the mistress of the house
6 Belt end in the form of a woman playing with a child.
7 A belt hanger. The upper part was rivetted to the belt, to sustain the weight of keys, toilet articles, etc. which were hung on long chains from the hinged end.
8 Casket key.
9 Door key.
10 Silver toothpick
11 Ivory hair parter. A detail.

12 Boxwood comb with inlaid decoration.
13 A fifteenth-century 'posy' (poetry) ring, with engraved motto. A outside inscription. B inside inscription. Such rings were often given as betrothal presents. The motto means 'in good faith'.
14 Portable writing set. The lids of the pencase and ink bottle slide along the cords.

A servant's tools and duties
15 Kitchen equipment, from a fifteenth-century woodcut.
16 A tub for 'bucking', a cleaning method used before soap was widely available. The folded clothes were kept apart by sticks, while lye, a cleaning fluid made from steeped wood ash, was poured through them.
17 Pounding washing with a wooden 'beatle'.
18 Beating the lumps out of a mattress.
19 Rocking the baby.
20 Bathing the master. Only rich people would have had such a grand bath.

New ideas, new worlds

Medieval scholarship was directed by the church. In the Dark Ages churchmen had been almost the only people who could read and write. Later they ran the schools and taught at the universities. The church taught that all knowledge came from God.

Petrarch, a fourteenth-century Italian poet, became interested in the questioning thought of Greek and Roman poets and philosophers. He started collecting manuscripts of their work and discussing them with other Italian scholars. This led them to the exciting idea that people could explore the universe and discover truths through the powers of their own reasoning.

In fifteenth-century Florence these scholars encouraged artists to imitate the arts of antiquity. The sculptor Donatello and the architect Brunelleschi went to Rome and grubbed about among the ruins to find models to copy. These inspired buildings and statues that were entirely new in style.

A leading citizen of Florence at this time, Cosimo de' Medici, was deeply interested in the new ideas and commissioned works of art and supported scholars. He asked Brunelleschi to design a house for him but rejected the plan as too grand. He asked Michelozzo to prepare something more modest and the result was the Palazzo Medici, the first private house since Roman times to be built with classical proportions.

The teachings of Plato

In 1439 Cosimo made Florence the host of a great meeting between the Pope and the Byzantine Emperor. The Emperor was accompanied by the Patriarch of Constantinople and many distinguished Greek scholars. Their coming had effects beyond any that Cosimo could have foreseen. The long beards and exotic clothes of the visitors, their Moorish servants and strange animals, amazed the townspeople and inspired painters. More importantly, the Greek scholars profoundly impressed Florentine thinkers. Cosimo listened to their discussions of the teachings of the Greek philosopher Plato and decided to create his own Platonic Academy. He encouraged the translation of Plato's works into Latin.

Plato had taught his pupils to find personal satisfaction by using their own abilities to the fullest extent. The idea that man could perfect himself through his own efforts in this world, rather than hoping to find perfection in the next, would have seemed nonsensical to a medieval mind but it was one that helped to shape the modern world.

1 These figures, from a marriage chest, are wedding guests, but even on normal occasions gold-embroidered brocades and enormous hats, formed around padded rolls, were worn by the rich merchant families. Lawmakers tried to limit such extravagence; there were fines for wearing too long a train. The woman's hat is made of feathers; the men on the right have parti-coloured hose.
2 A wooden hat box. The outside is stuccoed and gilded.
3–5 Women's hair was elaborately dressed.
6 Clogs were so high that ladies had to be supported by their maids.

Fifteenth-century Florentine craftsmanship
7 Golden rose made in Florence for Pius II. Each year the Pope made a gift of a golden rose. This one was presented to Siena.
8 Jewelled and enamelled belt-strap and buckle.
9 Gold and pearl pendant.
10 Ebony and ivory casket.

Cosimo de'Medici's villas

11 Cosimo de'Medici's country villa at Careggi, where the scholars of his 'Platonic Academy' met to discuss classical philosophy.

12 A fifteenth-century library. The books are displayed flat. Cosimo de'Medici formed a great book collection part of which later became the first public library in Europe.

13 The Palazzo Medici, designed for Cosimo by Michelozzo, and built 1446–60. Its balanced, ordered design, influenced by classical architecture, must have seemed strikingly new.

14 The Medici coat of arms.

15 Detail and section of the facade of the Palazzo Medici.

16 Relief in the church of Orsanmichele, Florence. Masons and sculptors were members of the same guild. Medieval people did not distinguish between craftsmen and artists.

Fresco painting

17 Cosimo's son Piero watches Benozzo Gozzoli decorating the chapel of the Palazzo Medici. Fresco is painted on fresh plaster, so the artist must work fast

before it dries. The work is done in sections. A pupil is plastering on the next area to be done. The artist will quickly resketch on it the guide lines which have been covered up. The main guide, or 'synopia', is visible on the underplaster.

Tempera painting

18 Back of a prepared panel braced with cross pieces.

19 The surface was sized, given several coats of gesso (chalk and size) and marked with the design. Before painting the gilding was done.

20 Grinding colours. These were mixed with water and egg.

21 An elaborate frame was made for the finished picture.

Oil painting

It used to be thought that oil painting was a fifteenth-century Flemish invention. However, oil was already in use in Italy for glazing tempera.

22 An oil painter at work. A and B oil palettes.

45

The science of mapmaking

One of the most influential of the ancient texts rediscovered at this time was the Geographica of Ptolemy, an Alexandrian astronomer and geographer of the 2nd century A.D. A copy had been brought to Florence from Constantinople in 1400. The maps in it were gridded with lines of longitude and latitude in a way unknown to medieval mapmakers. Since the development of the compass in the thirteenth century accurate coastal charts, based on seamen's observations, had been available, but there had been no way of defining a particular position anywhere in the world. Latitude and longitude made this possible. Florence became the centre for the study of cartography – the science of map making.

The Portuguese, a nation with a long tradition of sea trading, were especially interested in cartography. One of the four sons of the King of Portugal became known as Henry the Navigator because of his enthusiasm for exploring the unknown seas to the south of Portugal. He ordered maps and geographical material from Florence for the school of navigation he had funded at Sagres. Henry's motives, like those of many people at this time of new ideas, were a mixture of medieval and modern ways of thought. He wanted to wage a holy war against the Moslems and to convert the pagan inhabitants of new lands. He knew also that North African Moslem traders went south overland to a coast rich in ivory, spices, slaves and gold. He hoped to find this land and capture some of their trade by sea. He was also inspired by the excitement of the voyages down the African coast. The nautical charts at his school of navigation were revised and enlarged to record an expanding world. Later Portuguese rulers continued Henry's work, sending explorers down the seemingly endless African coast, until, in 1488, Bartolomeu Dias rounded its southernmost tip and the way to the spicelands of India was open.

The influence of exploration

The Portuguese explorations profoundly altered people's perceptions of the world and their position in it. Medieval notions of southern seas that steamed and boiled were shown to be false.

New maps, better navigational skills, and the sense of how much had already been achieved, gave rise to even bolder ideas. In 1474 the Italian mapmaker Toscanelli wrote about an idea in which he hoped to interest the King of Portugal – a shorter westward route to the spicelands. Because of an error originally made by Ptolemy he underestimated the size of the earth by many thousands of miles, one of history's most momentous mistakes, for it encouraged Christopher Columbus to make his historic journey.

Portuguese fifteenth-century costume
1 Coat of arms of the kingdom of Portugal.
2 A royal lady. Her elaborate overdress has a long train. The sides of the bodice are closed with buttoned tabs, showing the chemise below. Her hat combines the height of the popular 'henin' and the liripipe derived from the coiled-hood fashion.
3 A Portuguese sailor wearing a brigantine.
4 A young boy. His clothes follow adult fashion.
5 A nobleman in a full-skirted pourpoint and fringed cap.

Voyages in the names of Christ
6 A cruzado, a gold coin issued in 1457.
7 An iron nailhead, from a chest. It was originally gilded and bears the cross of the Order of Christ.
8 Portuguese silver-gilt cup.
9 Pillar with cross and arms of Portugal, erected by Diogo Caõ in 1483 on the coast of present-day Angola.
10 Silver-gilt reliquary casket.
11 Portuguese light armour devised for hot climates.
12 Fifteenth-century sword.

The Moorish caravel

13 Lustreware bowl showing ship with arms of Portugal on its sails, early fifteenth century.

14 The caravel, a ship of new design, light, narrow and three-masted, which the Portuguese used to explore the African coast. It was shallow enough to sail close inland, and on the homeward journey its lateen rig enabled it to sail into the prevailing winds.

15 The caravel re-rigged for the open sea. The square sails enabled it to travel fast, taking full advantage of following winds.

16 Fifteenth-century chart on oxhide, showing newly discovered African coast. The lines are compass bearings for the steersman to follow to reach his destination.

13

15

Afro-Portuguese ivories

Made for the Portuguese by African craftsmen.

25 Fork. The handle is decorated with a crocodile and a dog swallowing a snake.

26 Spoon with handle of entwined crocodiles.

27 Salt cellar representing two Portuguese dignitaries and their attendants. The lid of the salt containers is in the form of a ship with a man with a telescope in the crow's nest.

28 Hunting horn, with gold rim and mouthpiece.

29 Short stabbing spear used by Africans.

Fifteenth-century navigation

17 Hourglass used in measuring a ship's speed, judged by the time it took to pass a floating object thrown from its bows.

18 Seaman's astrolabe for measuring the altitude of the sun or pole star, to find out latitude at sea. 18a The central alidade, A, was rotated until the star could be seen through its sights. The pointers then showed the altitude, marked in degrees on the rim.

19 Seaman's quadrant. The plumbline's position on the arc indicated altitude when the sun was observed through the sights.

20 A crossstaff gave a more accurate reading on a heaving deck.

16

17

18

A

18a

19

20

The Portuguese in Africa

21 Map of the explorers' routes.

22 African bronze figure from the Yoruba city of Ife.

23 Bronze head of a king of Ife wearing the headdress of a sea-god.

24 Ivory mask, with iron inlay, worn on belt of the Oba, or King of Benin. It is decorated with Portuguese heads.

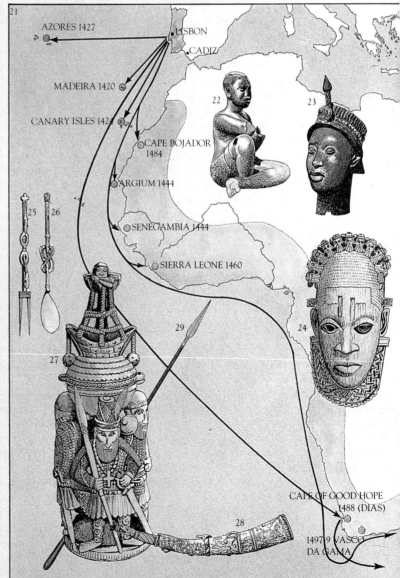

21

AZORES 1427

LISBON

CADIZ

MADEIRA 1420

22

23

CANARY ISLES 1424

CAPE BOJADOR 1484

ARGIUM 1444

SENEGAMBIA 1444

SIERRA LEONE 1460

25 26

29

27

24

28

CAPE OF GOOD HOPE 1488 (DIAS)

1497-9 VASCO DA GAMA

Booklist

KNIGHTS AND THE CRUSADES
The Book of the Medieval Knight by Stephen Turnbull (Arms and Armour Press 1985); *Medieval Warfare* by H. W. Koch (Bison Books 1978); *The Wars of the Crusades* by Terence Wise (Osprey Publishing 1978).

THE AGE OF GREAT CATHEDRALS
The Cathedral Builders by Jean Gimpel (Michael Russell 1983), *The Medieval Architect* by John Harvey (Wayland 1972); *The Sketchbook of Villehard de Honnecourt* edited by T. Bowie (Bloomington Indiana 1968).

THE VENICE OF MARCO POLO
Beyond the Horizon by Malcolm Ross Macdonald (Aldus Books 1971); *The Architectural History of Venice* by Deborah Howard (Batsford 1980); *China, Land of Discovery and Invention* by Robert K. G. Temple (Patrick Stephens 1986).

MEDIEVAL TECHNOLOGY
The Medieval Machine by Jean Gimpel (Gollancz 1977); *Medieval Technology and Social Change* by L. White (Oxford 1962); *The History of Technology* edited by C. Singer (Oxford 1956).

COUNTRY LIFE
The Luttrell Village by Sheila Sancha (Collins 1982); *Life on the English Manor* by H. S. Bennett (Cambridge University Press 1974); *A Historical Geography of Western Europe* by C. T. Smith (Longman 1967).

TRADE FAIRS AND MARKETS
Medieval Travellers by Margaret Wade Labarge (Hamish Hamilton 1982); *Fairs Past and Present* by Cornelius Walford (August Kelly N.Y. 1968); *The Champagne Fairs* C.I.B.A. Review No. 66.

ENTERTAINMENTS AND TOURNAMENTS
Sports and Pastimes of the People of England by J. Strutt (Methuen 1903); *The History of the Tournament in England and France* by Francis Henry Cripps-Day (Bernard Quaritch 1918); *Chivalry* by Michael Foss (Michael Joseph 1975)

PILGRIMS AND HOSPICES
Medieval Pilgrims by Gladys Scott Thompson (Longmans 1962); *Pilgrimages* by C. W. van Voorst van Beest (Lutterworth Press 1975); *A History of Medicine* by Brian Inglis (Weidenfeld & Nicolson 1965).

THE COURT OF BURGUNDY
The Golden Age of Burgundy by Joseph Calmette (Weidenfeld & Nicolson 1962); *The Court of Burgundy* by Otto Cartellieri (Routledge & Kegan Paul 1929), *Philip the Good* by Richard Vaughan (Longman 1970).

PROSPERITY IN THE TOWNS
Life in Medieval France by Joan Evans (Phaidon 1969); *Medieval People* by Eileen Power (Methuen 1986); *Women in Medieval Life* by Margaret Wade Labarge (Hamish Hamilton 1986).

NEW IDEAS, NEW WORLDS
The Renaissance Artist at Work by Bruce Cole (John Murray 1983); *The World of the Italian Renaissance* by E. R. Chamberlain (Allen & Unwin 1982); *Expanding Horizons* edited by Neville Williams (Weidenfeld & Nicolson 1974).